Photo by: Chelsie Hutto

Tribute to Paula Ramsey
"Mom"

Paula Ramsey, founder & owner of "A Lady's Day Out" has gone to be with her sweet savior. On August 22, 2000 she lost her battle with cancer. Mom's life was an example for many. We can all be assured her rewards were great and that the Father welcomed her home with open arms and a big "Thank you" for a life spent glorifying Him and bringing many into the Kingdom.

"A Lady's Day Out" was Mom's vision. As with most things in her life, she was willing to share this with me. We traveled from one exciting town to the next—finding treasures and experiencing so much together for more than 10 years. I was blessed to have shared these times with my mom and hold them dear in the quiet places of my heart.

The loss of my best friend, business partner and mother is great, and the pain is deep. Our family has lost our "rock," but our faith in the Lord is strong, and we take comfort in knowing we will someday join her again in heaven.

I will miss our adventures together, but I am thankful for the times we shared, and I feel blessed to have had a mom that others could only dream of. I have always been and will continue to be proud of my mother for her love of the Lord, her right choices, her ability to lead by example and the contributions she made here on earth. Mom had an unconditional love for all of her children, and as her daughter, I will miss that attribute the most.

We will continue to publish "A Lady's Day Out" books and see her vision through. A percentage of all book sales will go to charity in Mom's memory. Thank you for celebrating her memory with us. Each time you pick up this book or any of our others, we hope you think of Mom and her inspiration—Jesus Christ.

Jennifer "Jenni" Ramsey

Southern Pacific Railroad Depot, Edinburg, Texas
(See related story page 24.)

La Lomita Chapel
Mission, Texas
(See related story page 91.)

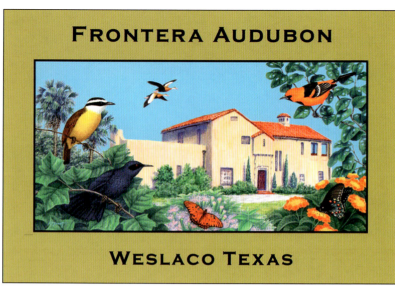

(See related story page 154.)

Weslaco, Texas
(See related story page 144.)

Broadway Hardware & Gifts
(See related story page 75.)

Celina's
(See related story page 71.)

Photo credit: Richard Stockton

Lynne Tate Real Estate
(See related story page 127.)

Super 8 Motel
(See related story page 51.)

South Padre Island
(See related story page 121.)

Pirates Landing
(See related story page 131.)

Sea Ranch
(See related story page 131.)

Imelda's Home Accessories & Gifts
(See related story page 19.)

Monrho's Gallery
(See related story page 16.)

A Lady's Day Out
in the Rio Grande Valley and South Padre Island

A Shopping Guide & Tourist Handbook

— *featuring* —

*Alamo City • Brownsville • Edinburg • Harlingen • Hidalgo
La Feria • Los Fresnos • McAllen • Mission • Pharr • Port Isabel
Port Mansfield • Raymondville • Reynosa • Rio Grande City
Roma • South Padre Island • Weslaco*

by **Jennifer Ramsey**

*Cover features the Roma-Ciudad Miguel Aleman Steel Suspension Bridge
(see related story on page 134)*

CREDITS

Editor/Author
Jennifer Ramsey

Director of Research & Sales
Jennifer Ramsey

Administrative Assistant
Kay Payne

Editor & Writer
Michelle Medlock Adams

Production
Beth Poulsen

Contributing Writers
Jenny Harper Nahoum
Sally Hall
Todd Winkler

Research & Sales
Tere Carter
Nancy Brummel
David Grindrod
Doris Phillips

Paid advertising by invitation only.

Printed in the United States of America
by Armstrong Printing Company, Austin, Texas

After enjoying this book, we are sure you will also love our other books:

AVAILABLE TITLES

A Lady's Day Out in the Texas Hill Country, Vol. II
A Lady's Day Out in Texas, Vol. II
A Lady's Day Out in Texas, Vol. III
A Lady's Day Out in Mississippi
A Lady's Day Out in Tulsa
A Lady's Day Out in Dallas / Arlington
A Kid's Day Out in the Dallas / Fort Worth Metroplex

Soon to be released:

– Fall 2003 –
A Lady's Day Out on Northwest Florida's
Emerald Coast

– Winter 2003 –
A Lady's Day Out in Nashville, Tennessee
& Surrounding Areas

TO ORDER CALL 1-888-860-ALDO (2536)

Dear Adventurer,

If you are reading this book chances are you are an 'Adventurer.' An 'Adventurer' is a person with a sense of adventure and a curiosity for new and exciting places, people and experiences—both long and short distances. All of the Lady's Day Out books appeal to that sense of adventure and cater to the natural curiosity in all of us.

A Lady's Day Out, Inc., would like to share this gift of the perfect combination between work and travel with our loyal following of readers.

In an effort to expand our coverage area we are looking for adventurous travelers who would like to help us find the greatest places to include in our upcoming editions of A Lady's Day Out. This is a wonderful opportunity to travel and explore some of the best destination cities in the United States.

If you would like more information we would love to hear from you. You may call A Lady's Day Out, Inc. at 1-888-860-ALDO (2536) or e-mail us at www.aladysdayout.com.

Best wishes and keep on exploring, from all of us at A Lady's Day Out, Inc.

Table of Contents

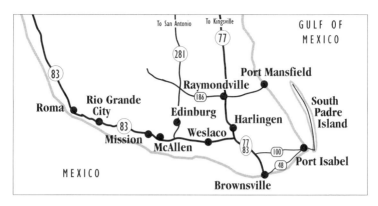

Introduction

For many years, the Texas Rio Grande Valley and South Padre Island have been a "well-kept secret" from many, including myself. Those who have discovered this wonderful part of Texas rich in history, charm and culture, have kept it very "hush-hush." I don't believe these "Keepers of the Secret" were being selfish; I think they were just savoring the unspoiled charm as long as they could.

After spending the past four seasons in "The Valley," as the locals call it, I have come to know and appreciate this part of Texas and am excited to share it with you.

Influences from Mexico are gloriously apparent in every inch of The Valley. And, the people who live there are warm and hospitable—quite proud of their heritage and culture. Many residents of The Valley are direct descendants of Mexicans who came to the United States during the first wave of immigration, bringing with them very strong religious roots, and planting those roots into their new surroundings. In San Juan, you will find the "Basilica Of Our Lady Of San Juan Del Valle-National Shrine." Placed here in 1949, it was miraculously unharmed in 1970 when a pilot crashed his plane directly into the shrine. Thousands of tourists visit this landmark today.

Everything from sleepy fishing villages and communities reminiscent of the Old West to Padre Island resorts and towns with trendy metropolitan shopping can be found in "The Valley." Make a special trip to the Rio Grande Valley and South Padre Island. Prepare yourself for relaxation, historic sites, great shopping and wonderful people. Have fun and don't keep "the Secret" to yourself—tell a friend!

Jennifer "Jenni" Ramsey

RIO GRANDE VALLEY

It is a place where nature and wildlife blend perfectly with heritage and history, where cultures come together as easily as sweet cream in a hot cup of coffee, and where the warmth and friendliness of the people welcome and charm all who visit their blessed land. It is the Rio Grande Valley, filled with swaying palms, pristine sandy shores, sparkling waters, lush citrus groves, exotic wildlife, and very charming people. And that's only the beginning! This "Magic Valley" invites visitors from around the world to bask in the warmth of the mild winters and to explore its tropical paradise, from the scenic back roads and wildlife refuges to the golden sands of the Gulf. Be warned though, many who visit never leave. The Valley can be mysterious and captivating, with a charisma and laid-back lifestyle that, like a colorful Mexican serape, seems to wrap itself around everyone who visits.

The fascinating history of the Valley encompasses Spanish conquistadors, Franciscan padres, fierce tribes of Indians and Mexican banditos. Its present-day description includes destination beaches and world-class fishing, limitless tourism opportunities, unrivaled shopping experiences, and more fun than you can even imagine! Mexico, just minutes away, has lent its colorful and festive, yet easy way of life to the surrounding Valley towns, blending the cultures through the years into a warm, friendly lifestyle that encompasses the best of two nations. In fact, the people are the single most important asset to this part of Texas. You will find them to be happy and content, friendly and welcoming, and extremely proud of their beautiful Valley. Everyone seems to smile all of the time, carrying within them a peaceful contentment to be alive in such a beautiful place. You'll see this on the faces of the children and their abuelitas (grandmothers) in the border towns, in the sun-wrinkled grins of the Gulf's fishermen, and in the delight of a birder spotting a Chachalaca! This contentment and happiness is an intangible, yet very strong, enticement to linger in the Valley. You will actually feel the everyday stress and hurriedness of life disappear as you experience the colors, flavor and spirit of the magical Rio Grande Valley.

DOWN MEXICO WAY!

Just a two-step away from the Valley you'll find the charming, romantic, and exotic Mexico, luring visitors across the Rio Grande with its colorful culture, wonderful shopping, and sizzling fajitas! The sights and smells of this southern neighbor are like nowhere else on earth. It is as ancient and exotic a place as you will ever experience. Strolling mariachis entertain visitors with their traditional songs and music; diners sip frosty mugs of margaritas; and vendors line the streets with their intriguing wares. You'll see leather goods; wicker baskets; cowboy hats and sombreros; hand-woven blankets and silver jewelry. Liquor shops and pharmacies are very popular, as are the handmade crafts and Mexican folkart. Aromas of roasted corn, fried tortillas, and freshly baked pastries entice you to stop and taste the specialties, but just catch your breath, because you won't want to miss a minute of the sidewalk menagerie of Mexican culture. There are 11 current border crossings along the three border counties of the Rio Grande Valley, including: Falcon Dam/Nuevo Guerrero; Roma/Cuidad Aleman; Rio Grande City/Cuidad Carmargo; Los Ebanos/Diaz Ordas; McAllen-Hidalgo/Reynosa; Pharr/Reynosa; Progreso/Nuevo Progreso; The Free Trade Bridge; and Brownsville/Matamoros. We found that not only in Mexico, but also in the border towns and even throughout many of the larger Valley cities, the prices are comparably lower than other parts of Texas, so you'll find wonderful bargains. It is a shopper's dream!

WINTER TEXANS

The semi-tropical climate and delightfully warm winters lure a wonderful group of people from across the nation to leave their coats at home, dig their toes into the sand, and as they say in Texas, "stay awhile." They have acquired the name Snow Birds or Winter

Texans, but the Valley calls them "family!" This pilgrimage begins every year from November through March. Just like the birds, convoys of RVs and campers head south. The Valley has become a second home to hundreds of thousands of visitors who have fallen in love with this tropical playground of Texas. As you can imagine, these winter visitors have a significant impact on the area and its economy, and the Valley works harder and harder to make their stay as much fun as possible. Melting away memories of dreary winters are social gatherings, golfing, dancing, wonderful shopping, museum browsing, and fiestas created especially for them, but their favorite things about the valley winters are just the clear skies, and bright sun-filled days. By the end of March, when the wildflowers begin to bloom, the Winter Texans head home, with the palms waving a gentle goodbye. They'll be back, because nothing beats the warm and friendly welcome they get from the beautiful Rio Grande Valley. Like them, you will love the startling beauty of the land, the wide array of fascinating historic sites; natural wonders; cultural attractions; and nature "as big as all outdoors."

A VALLEY "FOR THE BIRDS"

Even if Old Man Winter never visits the Valley, furry, feathered creatures sure do. Birdwatching in the Rio Grande is legendary, with sun-drenched landscapes perfect for observing some of nature's most beautiful and fascinating birds and butterflies. Because the Valley is situated at the crossroads of two main migratory flyways between North and South America, more than 500 species of birds and 300 varieties of butterflies are spotted in the Valley each year. The coast of South Texas offers huge masses of marsh and water, lots of sunshine, and plenty of things a bird likes to eat. This might just be the reason so many migrate to the Valley, and the reason so many birders flock here to see them. Texas claims to be the nation's top birding destination, and according to Cheryl LaBerge of the Harlingen Area Chamber of Commerce, birding brings in more than $100 million each year to the Valley. Texas is even home to a parrot population that was created through the years by escaped pets. The "red-heads," as they are known have brilliant green bodies with a Lucille Ball topknot, and can be found nesting at night in the city of McAllen. The Boca Chica Wetlands near Brownsville afford visitors glimpses of falcons and pelicans that frequent the lomas or elevated islands, and the Santa Ana National Wildlife Refuge, south of Alamo City, boasts more species of birds than any other spot in the United States. This 2,088-acre refuge attracts birders from around the world. And, it has a world-famous mascot, "Chachalaca," whose "call" sounds just like its name! So grab your binoculars, and get ready for the most exciting birding you can imagine.

THE SPARKLING GULF

Okay, shop 'til you drop. Add to your "list" of exotic birdsighting. Tour the scenic roads that lead to Mexico. And, do-si-do all night long, but don't forget to enjoy the beautiful unspoiled beaches of the gulf. They are the perfect playground for sailing; fishing; windsurfing; dolphin watching; horseback riding; or just soaking in the sun. Located at the tropical tip of Texas, and only 25 miles north of the Mexican border, South Padre Island is one of the nation's premiere beaches and vacation resorts. From sunrise to sunset, from early morning fishing trips to cocktails on the deck of a rustic wharf, this is the ideal vacation spot. You can pick your favorite water transportation, from amphibious vehicles and catamarans to a gentle horseback ride, splashing in the surf. Make your trip to the coast as adventurous or romantic as you wish.

If fishing is your favorite sport, get ready to bend your pole along the surf, out in the bay, or on a deep-sea fishing trip. You will also love the idea that whatever you catch at the end of the day, you can have for dinner! Many of the great restaurants along the water will "cook your catch!" Tour the island and its historic neighbor Port Isabel, and learn the exciting history of its early Spanish settlers. If you're a golfer, you'll want to test your game at one of the many championship courses. If you're into culture, you'll want to visit the many museums and nature parks. There are so many wonderful things to do and see and taste along the gulf coast, you'll find yourself needing just one more day, just one more cast, just one more dive, just one more sunset. The gulf is a place you will remember forever.

"TRUE RIO GRANDE VALLEY GEMS—SPECIAL PEOPLE WITH SPECIAL BUSINESSES"

There are so many wonderful people in the Rio Grande Valley. It's as if God put the warmest, friendliest and most talented folks in this tropical part of Texas. Just one visit to any of the towns featured in this book, and you'll fully appreciate the people behind the businesses. Every person has a story, and we wanted to share those with you in the following pages. A few of the extraordinary people we met along the way have been highlighted in this section because of their uniqueness. So we challenge you to spend some time visiting with the folks who own the restaurants, the retail shops and others. Get to know them, and you're just bound to make some lifelong friends.

ARMANDO DUARTE

Armando Duarte grew up knowing the smell of leather, feeling its smoothness, and seeing it being shaped and stitched into things of beauty. He spent his childhood days in his grandfather's leather shop in Mexico, learning from the master boot maker, the art that would one day be his future. His grandfather made saddles, belts, and boots—everything shaped by hand. When his Uncle Abraham Rios came to the United States to open a leather store, Armando would visit, and continued to learn the art of tooling fine leather. Finally in 1960, Armando became an American citizen and settled in the town of Raymondville. He continued to work under the tutelage of his Uncle Abraham, spending two or three years in each department of the store until his uncle's death in 1978.

Armando tried to carry on the business until a mild heart attack forced him to take it easy, but his loyal customers encouraged him to continue the tradition he had learned so long ago. In 1982 Armando opened his own shop, and his business has been growing for more than 20 years. Customers travel from great distances to have boots made by Armando, including movie stars, political giants, and famous ranchers.

The entire Duarte family has been involved in making Armando's Boot Company a great success. Elva works right beside her husband, and their son Armando Jr. has also become a gifted boot maker. The poignant story of the Duarte family is one that parallels the history of the Valley itself. It is one of people who persevere through the hardships of life and draw proudly upon their heritage and skills learned from their ancestors. With a "can-do" determination that embodies the feisty spirit of the Rio Grande, the Armando Duarte family has succeeded in keeping alive the wonderful art of boot making. You will enjoy getting to know this softspoken gentleman and his family. You'll also appreciate their strength of character that is so prevalent throughout this warm and wonderful Valley.

ELIDA GUAJARDO

When Elida Guajardo planned her gift shop in La Feria, she wanted to travel into the interior of Mexico to seek out unique and special treasures. This took some doing, and a lot of begging. Because they had never ventured into the Mexican interior, her husband Silvestre was a little apprehensive, and it turned out, with good reason. They got lost in the mountains the first day! (To tell you what a wonderful man he is, the words "I told you so" were never spoken!) Things just happen for good reasons, because during this rather scary adventure, the two happened upon something that would forever change their lives. They found a beautiful natural stone they had never seen before, and made immediate plans to return soon to purchase it. Elida found that the further into Mexico they ventured, the more unique treasures they found—items she knew would be wonderful in her store. She has selected pieces that are truly works of art—soft and supple leather purses, crystal and wrought iron candelabras, and one-of-a-kind pieces of jewelry.

Elida and Silvestre are a delightful and very talented couple who work side-by-side in their shared businesses, Ele's Gift Shop, and Cantera Rancho Alegre.

"I don't understand how people can say that they can't work with their husbands," says Elida. "Silvestre and I work every day together, sharing our plans and ideas about what we will do, how we will grow, and how we will offer special things for our customers."

Not only do *they* work together, but the entire family is involved in every aspect of the store. Their two sons are learning every part of the business, with a desire to follow in the footsteps of their talented father. Silvestre's creations from the natural Mexican stone include incredible hand-carved pillars, tables, benches, birdbaths and statues. Much of the stone has been used inside the store in unusual ways such as molding, and framing. When asked about the name Cantera Rancho Alegre, we learned that Cantera is Spanish for "natural stone," and Rancho Alegre means "joyful ranch." This Rancho Alegre was the first place they found the stone they now use, so "joyful ranch natural stone" became the meaning behind their new business. You won't find anything like the unusual items here. The one-of-a-kind pieces are truly extraordinary.

Elida told us that her biggest desire in having her own store, is to find things that will become the most treasured items in someone's home.

"It is easy to go right to the border, or to the U.S. markets to shop," she says, " but going the extra distance, to places where artists create from the heart, I find things that no one else will have."

This husband and wife team exemplifies the strong tie to country, tradition, and family so prevalent in the Valley, and is the perfect example of what hard work, determination, and a strong spirit will create. In them you will find a combination of sweetness and strength, humility and pride, but most of all a love for each other, their family, and their beautiful Rio Grande Valley.

GLORIA BOWLING & RUTHIE EWERS

Glory B … I used to hear my grandmother say this when she wanted to express complete amazement at something. The name is absolutely perfect for this extraordinary Harlingen patio and gift shop, and for the two amazing friends who own it. Ruthie Ewers met Gloria Bowling when she hired her to decorate her home. The two hit it off immediately, and realized that during the process of "re-decorating" they had not had a single disagreement—very unusual. They became friends, and soon after that, business partners, in one of the Valley's most unusual and successful businesses. Their desire, as Gloria explains, is to bring to the people of the Valley, things they will not easily find, or things they have only seen in magazines, and cannot imagine being able to own. "Many of the people here never leave the Valley, and so do not have the chance to discover new markets of home and patio accessories," she says. "We love being able to open up new opportunities and ideas to our friends and customers, to bring the world to them, and to help make it more beautiful."

When they decided to look for a building for their store, Gloria kept dragging Ruthie to this greasy, "horrendous" old tire shop on the outskirts of Harlingen at 2901 S. 77 Sunshine Strip. "I don't know," said Ruthie. But with Gloria's experienced decorator's eye, and a "feeling" about the place she couldn't explain, she said, "I know." With lots of hard work and their incredible imaginations, their merchandise now fills four rooms, an upstairs, two huge patios, and the outside yard. They meant to start small, but Ruthie does not do things "small." As a woman who had built an incredibly successful Dallas advertising company from her kitchen table, she likes "big," and knows how to make it happen. Even with her involvement on the boards of the Harlingen Chamber of Commerce, the American Heart, and the Salvation Army, and chairperson of the Harlingen Proud Board as well, she spends much of her time as the buyer for the store, (and loves it!)

This amazing duo are exact opposites, which is probably what makes them such great friends and partners. Ruthie is outgoing, adventurous, and never finds an obstacle she can't conquer. Gloria is low key, quiet-spoken, and very artistic. Both are friendly, genuine, and fun-loving, and the folks of Harlingen have fallen in love with them. In fact, the gals can be heard every Monday over KTEX Radio, chatting, laughing, and sharing "people news" or talking about the community events. The ladies of Glory B's stand out in the business world as examples of how to turn vision into reality, of how sometimes two completely different personalities are the perfect combination for success, and that staying grounded in community and tradition offers remarkable, life-changing opportunities. That sometimes when you grab on and do what you have dreamed, the result can only be described as … "glory b!"

SHIRLEY & RISE ATKINS

If you are lucky enough to be able to watch one of their rehearsals, you will be enthralled with two of Weslaco's most well-known and beloved women, Shirley Atkins and Rise Atkins Morris. Shirley and Rise are more than just mother and daughter. They have been an integral part of one of Weslaco's most beloved historical attractions, the Tower Theatre of Weslaco. In 1969, the city water tower was in danger of being destroyed when new facilities were built. With the vision and determination of many of the townspeople (including Shirley) the tower was saved and renovated into a "Theatre in the Round," which has delighted audiences for more than 30 years!

In the early days of the theatre, Shirley taught elementary music classes, and became integrally involved with the theatre's productions. As a Valley native, she graduated from Pan American University. Daughter Rise (pronounced Rees-ah) has a Masters Degree of Education in Counseling and Guidance from The University of Texas-Pan American and a B.A. in Mass Communications. She literally "grew up" in the theatre, and points to a corner of the theatre where she says, "I used to sit by the lights and do my homework during rehearsals." Taking in all of the sights, sounds, smells, and excitement of the theatre from such an early age definitely impacted Rise's future, because she (like her mother) directs and stars in many of the theatre productions.

Shirley retired from the public school system after 38 years. Now you'll find her behind the theatre piano as the musical director for the Tower's many wonderful productions. She has been on the board of the Mid Valley Civic Theatre since its beginning in

1969, and has been directing with her daughter for the last 21 years.

Both ladies love performing at the Tower. They love the warmth and intimacy of the small theatre, and say that they feel a wonderful connection to the audience. All of the cast members are volunteers from the Valley, which means they are working with friends and family. From ages 7 to 70, the entire cast has fun together, and it is obvious in every performance.

What makes these two women so special is that they absolutely love what they do. They might complain about the details involved in directing—casting plays, missing actors, long rehearsals, finding costumes, and building sets, but they smile as they do, because they love every minute of it. They are talented, energetic, resourceful, and committed to their art and their hometown. By using their many talents, and (it seems) every minute of their spare time, they have contributed tremendously in making the Tower Theatre of Weslaco and the Mid Valley Civic Theatre the success it is today. These are definitely two of the Valley's "Grand Ladies!"

BIRDING BED & BREAKFASTS
OF THE RIO GRANDE VALLEY

After a day of shopping and exploring, kick back and prop your feet up in one of the comfortable, serene Birding Bed and Breakfasts of the Rio Grande Valley.

Your first stop on the drive to the Rio Grande Valley along US Hwy 77 is the ranching town of Sarita—home to warm and inviting Great Kiskadee House B&B. 361-294-5722

Continue south and encounter The Inn at El Canelo just north of Raymondville, which is the home of Armando's Custom Boot Company. The inn is on a wildlife-rich ranch famous for great cooking, birding, deer, and spring flowers. 956-689-5042

Near Harlingen, whose main downtown street is lined with charming antique shops, Vieh's B&B is home to tropical trees, excellent cooking and Mexico bird tours. 956-425-4651

Travel east towards the coast, and outside of Los Fresnos you will find the impressive Inn at Chachalaca Bend. This Inn is set on an oxbow lake and its tropical gardens and woods attract both birds and guests. 956-233-1180

The Port Isabel/South Padre Island area is a shoppers delight. The charming Brown Pelican Inn, which offers very tasty breakfasts, overlooks the sparkling Laguna Madre with its beautiful sunsets. 956-761-2722

Also on sunny South Padre, Casa de Siesta offers oversized rooms—with stained glass windows—surrounding a courtyard with a fountain and a lush tropical garden. 956-761-5656

Traveling west on US Hwy 83 you come to the mid-Valley. Just a short walk from the world-famous Santa Ana National Wildlife Refuge is comfortable, quiet, well-appointed Casa Santa Ana. This lovely B&B is also a short drive from the international bridge at Progreso and great Mexico shopping. 956-783-5540

Nearby in Alamo is the historic Alamo Inn Suites, which has comfortable antique furnishings, a birding bookshop and a great restaurant next door. 956-782-9912

Near the city of Mission and Bentsen Rio Grande State Park, Suzanne welcomes guests at the exquisite Indian Ridge B&B and equestrian center. This B&B is the closest to the international bridge at Hidalgo. 956-519-3305

Visit www.rgv-bedandbreakfast.com online, for more information or reservations.

DISCOVER BROWNSVILLE

It is the perfect place for a "two nation-vacation," with its one set of roots planted deeply in Mexico, the other firmly in Texas. The ethnic culture is evident throughout the entire city, pulsating with South Texas charm and all the flavor of ancient Mexico. Steeped in the heritage of the Rio Grande delta, Brownsville is a city of "unhurried" southwestern charm, yet with a definite sense of adventure.

Brownsville is a seaport and port of entry from Matamoros, Mexico, bringing ships from all parts of the world to the tip of Texas. It was first established as Fort Taylor, after General Zachary Taylor, but was changed to Fort Brown in 1846. It was named for Major Jacob Brown who was fatally wounded defending the fort in a six-day cannonade. Fort Brown is also the first federal fort in Texas. The original fort is now the site of the University of Texas at Brownsville and Texas Southmost College, as well as the Fort Brown Memorial Golf Course. Through the years Brownsville has grown from a tiny frontier town into an international center of commerce, all the while retaining its wonderful small-town charm and festive traditions. You'll find Brownsville to be a tropical environment of palm trees; vibrant bougainvilleas; exotic birds; colorful sunsets; and gentle coastal breezes. Its warm sub-tropical climate, lush landscapes, abundant wildlife and birding opportunities keep visitors "flocking" to this colorful city.

BROWNSVILLE HERITAGE

The bricklaying maestros from Mexico were responsible for building much of Brownsville. You'll see unique cornices and

Spanish styles of architecture throughout the city, even in new construction. A majestic tribute to Gothic architecture can be found in the historic Immaculate Conception Cathedral, which was built in 1854 by French Oblate missionaries. In fact, you may still attend Spanish mass there. Catholicism came to the Rio Grande Valley with the early pioneers and the Oblates of Mary Immaculate during the 1800s. Robert E. Lee introduced the Episcopal Church to the region during the latter part of that century, and many other religious orders can also trace their roots to Brownsville's early days. This history of religion and faith has influenced the growth of the city, and is an integral part of its heritage and definition.

Brownsville is a city of museums and historic sites which interpret its past so vividly. One site that you must not miss is the Historic Brownsville Museum, which is housed in the restored Southern Pacific Railroad Depot. Make sure you see the notable artifacts displayed in the San Pedro Motor Chapel. This was a mobile, wooden altar, which was transported to the area ranches for mass in the early 1900s by the Oblate of Mary Immaculate fathers. Also in this museum, you'll see the 1870 Baldwin wood-burning railroad locomotive, the last of its kind in the world. This tiny "choo-choo" train chugged the 22 miles from Brownsville to Port Isabel from 1872 to 1918, and was the Valley's only way to distribute steamship cargo from eastern ports.

Finally, painting a beautiful picture of bygone years, the Old City Cemetery is a true monument to the people and events of Brownsville's early days. The ornate monuments and above ground crypts are engraved with epitaphs that tell stories about the early pioneers and veterans from the Civil War and early American conflicts. The historic cemetery provides a connection with Brownsville's heritage sites.

FIESTAS, SPECIAL EVENTS, AND ATTRACTIONS

Brownsville's border culture springs to life during the many festivals and events throughout the year. Charro Days Fiesta, which is usually held at the end of February, is a twin-city celebration with neighboring Matamoros that includes music, parades, folkloric dancing, mariachis, and of course, food! The Commemorative Air Fiesta is held in March, which brings vintage and military aircraft to the skies. And, in July, the Gulf Shrimp Festival celebrates the area's shrimping industry with various activities.

Talk to the animals! The Gladys Porter Zoo is Brownsville's internationally famous botanical and zoological park, a collection of some of the world's most rare and endangered species of animals. This visitor-friendly oasis is home to more than 1,500 species of mammals, birds, reptiles, fish, and insects in natural settings. Indoor and outdoor exhibits house animals from Asia Indo-Australia, Africa, and the Americas. The zoo spans 31 acres, and has the look of a tropical sanctuary, complete with native palms, rushing waterfalls, and lush bamboo. You can take a walking tour in less than an hour, but if you're like me, you'll want to linger at the favorites! One of the most popular exhibits is the gorilla habitat. Eight western lowland gorillas romp on rocky islands, while the youngsters play tag among the trees. There is always a crowd here! Kids also will love seeing the "double-wattled cassowary," a large, flightless bird from Australia that looks like it stepped right out of Jurassic Park. A dagger-like claw on the middle toe of each foot makes it one of the most dangerous of all birds. The zoo director tells us that they rarely reproduce in zoos, because they can't even stand one another! For more information, call 956-546-2177.

FOR THE BIRDS!

As in most of the Valley, Brownsville is an internationally acclaimed birding destination. It is the southern beginning of the Texas Coastal Birding Trail and part of the annual Great Texas Birding Classic. Popular birding sites around Brownsville include Tamaulipas Crow Park, the Sabal Palm Audubon Sanctuary, and the Boca Chica dunes and wetlands. The Red-crowned Parrot is the city's official bird, but one of the most entertaining might be the "Chachalaca" who very loudly states its given name. You will actually hear it sing cha-cha-la-ca, in a loud, penetrating call.

For more information on Brownsville, call the Brownsville Convention and Visitors Bureau at 956-546-3721 or visit www.brownsville.org.

Brownsville Fairs Festivals & Fun

February
   Charro Days

March
   Commemorative Air Fiesta

April
   Annual Student Int'l Art Show

June
   Expo Fiesta (Matamoros)
   Starlight Safari Sleepover

July
   Fourth of July Celebration
   Brownsville International Birding Festival
   Expo Fiesta (Matamoros)
   Gulf Shrimp Festival

September
   Dieciseis de Septiembre Celebration (Matamoros)

October
   "Boo at the Zoo" Gladys Porter Zoo
   Annual Latin Jazz Festival

November
   Christmas Tree Lighting Ceremony

December
   "Zoo Nights & Lights" Gladys Porter Zoo
   Annual Christmas Parade

Art Galleries

MONRHO'S GALLERY

The historic home at 319 E. Elizabeth is listed on the National Historic Register, and is a Brownsville Heritage Site. It's a beautiful backdrop for the unique and wonderful artwork and gifts at Monrho's Gallery. The collection of hand-crafted items and collectibles include table linens by April Cornell; leather goods by Mulholand Brothers; and Stark rugs. From baby to bride, you'll find a plethora of exciting items  such as: stained glass, stoneware, jewelry, woven shawls, bar tools, vintage purses, cookbooks, and hand-made ceramics. There is both a baby and bridal registry, invitations for special occasions, and pretty wrapping papers and packaging for your gifts. Owners, Rhonda Rodriguez and Monica Davis were raised in Brownsville, and they love being able to offer their hometown such a unique shopping experience. The store is open Tuesday-Friday 10 am-6 pm and Saturday until 5 pm. Call 956-982-8995. *(Color picture featured in front section of the book.)*

Fashion & Accessories

When a heavy storm caused the roof to collapse on the Gelfer family's shoe store, it only served as a catalyst to rebuild and expand. Today, Country Casuals, located at "The Corner on Boca Chica" at 2200 Boca Chica Blvd, is one of Brownsville's landmark stores, and a first choice for locals and visitors alike. David and Jayme Gelfer founded Country Casuals in 1967. Today, this beautiful 8,000-square-foot clothing store anchors a 60,000-square-foot shopping center owned by the family. Daughter Robin and son-in-law Mike Pierce joined the business in the 1980s and currently run Country Casuals with David and Jayme. The architecture and design of the store are beautiful. It is decorated with stained glass, and antique pieces the Gelfers have collected. Country Casuals offers all the services of a fine specialty shop—free alterations, free gift-wrapping, layaway, and in-house charge accounts. You'll find ladies shoes and handbags; sportswear; daytime and evening wear for both misses and contemporary customers; jewelry; gifts; and children's clothing. Stop by! You'll love the personal attention to your individual needs. The store is open Monday-Saturday 10 am-8 pm. Call 956-546-3771.

Florists

ROSENBAUM FLOWERS & GIFTS

Their names are Viola and Yolanda Rosenbaum. The name Rosenbaum means "tree of roses," and the names Viola and Yolanda come from a word that means "violet." Even better, Rosenbaum Flowers and Gifts is located at 874 Hortencia Blvd, and the word "Hortencia" means "hydrangea." It seems that they were destined to be florists! Both Viola and Yolanda are "Texas Master Florists," certified by the state of Texas and their work is a testament to this honor. Rosenbaum's has been in Brownsville for more than 25 years and the arrangements and gift baskets are works of art! Hours are Monday-Friday 9 am-6 pm and Saturday 9 am-3 pm. Call 956-542-7493.

Gifts & Home Décor

Casa Antigua, 2200 Boca Chica Blvd in Brownsville, offers Old World elegance. Owner and artist Rosario Gonzalez designs more than 450 metal pieces manufactured and sold in the store and through upscale catalogs. You'll find charger plates, candleholders, pot racks, fireplace screens and barstools. High-end furniture and accessories from India, Indonesia, Pakistan, Morocco and Mexico are all hand-crafted, one-of-a-kind pieces. Hours are Monday-Saturday 10 am-6 pm. Call 956-504-0999.

Imelda's
Home Accessories & Gifts

After selling insurance for 21 years, Imelda Swetnam was definitely ready for something different, something fun, and something that would allow her to use the creative part of her personality! She opened Imelda's Home Accessories & Gifts at 5460 N. Paredes Line Road in Brownsville, and has absolutely loved her exciting new career!

She carries very unique and interesting things for the home or winter bungalow, and if she doesn't have it, she will find it! Customers tell us that she personally takes care of them, and goes out of her way to make their shopping experience wonderful. We loved the wonderful selection of beautiful pillows for every room in the house, and the unique tabletop decorations. There are special items for every décor. The shop is open Monday-Saturday 10 am-6 pm. For more information, call 956-546-4120. *(Color picture featured in front section of the book.)*

SECOND THOUGHT

Although this store originated as a consignment shop more than 16 years ago, it has evolved into a wonderful combination of old and new for the home. It is a family-owned-and-operated business where personal attention and customer service is number one. You'll find everything from stationary to dining tables here! Second Thought is located at 2200 Boca Chica Blvd in Brownsville in "The Corner Shopping Center." Shop here first for the best prices. You'll certainly have no "second thoughts" because owner Myrna Hunter's knowledge of antiques and quality décor is evident in every room. Hours are Monday-Saturday 10 am-6 pm. Call 956-541-7423.

CREATIVE INTERIORS

Jeanne Ehlert was a stay at home mom who spent years making her home a beautiful and wonderful place for her family, as well as designing and building sensational sets for Children's Church. She made her "dream come true" when she opened the "dream of a store," Creative Interiors at 1940 Pecan Street, Suite D in Brownsville. Every wall is painted in a different faux finish, displaying the artistic services offered by Jeanne and her talented staff, and the floors are painted as trails that lead to wonderful rooms  filled with beautiful gifts. She carries several lines of blinds and shutters for custom window treatments; new and antique furniture; lamps; candles; pillows; and more. Whether you are tackling a large decorating project, making a few improvements, or looking for the perfect gift, be sure to visit Creative Interiors. You'll get wonderful, free consultations for all of your interior design needs. Call 956-504-5600.

Hotels

RESIDENCE INN BY MARRIOTT

The Residence Inn at 3975 N. Expwy 83 in Brownsville was designed to make you feel at home for a day, a week, or even a month. The suites give you 50 percent more space than a traditional hotel room, and all accommodations have a fully-equipped kitchen including a coffee maker; cooking and eating utensils; dishes and glassware; a dishwasher, a microwave and a refrigerator. You'll also enjoy a delicious full complimentary breakfast each morning so you'll be ready for anything the Valley has to offer. The Inn also offers a fitness center and a spa, a beautiful pool, and if needed, a meeting and banquet facility. For room rates or reservations, call 956-350-8100.

Restaurants & Bakeries

If you are hungry for delicious seafood, we know the perfect place! The Blue Shell, 2500 N. Hwy 77/83 in Brownsville, is an unusual mix of Mexican and American cuisine that completely changes the traditional ideas about seafood. You will, of course, find the expected fried, grilled, and baked fish, shrimp, and oysters, as well as deliciously spicy gumbo, but try the unusual Mexican twist to seafood in the restaurant's signature dishes. Daily specials include Tabasqueno, Veracruz, and Chipolte Fish, with sauces as spicy and exciting as their names, or a Seafood Chile Relleno. Two all-time customer favorites are the Crab Enchiladas (mild and creamy,) and the Shrimp Sombrero. Delicious! Restaurant hours are Monday-Thursday and Sunday 11 am-10 pm, Friday and Saturday until 11 pm. Be sure to visit the McAllen locations at 4009 N. 23rd Street and 3817 N. 10th Street, as well as the Harlingen location at 1306 Ed Carey Drive. Call 956-504-3777 or visit www.theblueshell.com.

Amaretti
Original Recipe Cakes

Amaretti Cakes has a way of making the most special day even more special. Each cake is specially designed just for your event Whether it's a birthday, an anniversary or a "just because cake," the bakers at Amaretti take the time to get to know each new customer so the cake can be as unique as its recipient.

For the brides-to-be, Amaretti has a beautiful selection of wedding cakes and offers a step-by-step program to make the big day even more stunning.

Feel free to browse the store's display of birthday and quinceanera cakes, each more colorful and original than the next—not to mention delicious! There are 33 flavors in all!

Located on 3014 International Blvd in Brownsville, Amaretti Cakes is open Monday-Saturday 9 am-7 pm and Sunday noon-4 pm. Call 956-986-0501.

Salons & Spas

"We enjoy helping people look and feel great!" Zaira Ruiz shares. That is the goal of the entire staff at The Hair'Em His & Hers Salon at 2200 Boca Chica Blvd, Suite 108 in Brownsville. Recognizing a demand for qualified color specialists, Zaira completed extensive courses in color and color correction enabling her to offer excellent service to her growing client base. She uses products such as Decleor, Redken, and Schwarzkopf, a product containing nettle and bamboo extract, sunflower oil, and sabal palm extract. This all-inclusive hair and body salon offers cuts, styles, color, and perms; spa manicures and spa pedicures; full body waxing; and professional facials and makeup. Take advantage of the wonderful massage therapy, full body exfoliation and polish too! A light lunch is provided with various spa packages. Hours are Monday-Friday 10 am-6 pm and Saturday 10 am-5 pm. Call 956-542-0968.

Special Events, Groups, Attractions & Entertainment

Anna and Cesar Perez grew up in Brownsville, and are raising their own children there. The only thing missing, they thought, was a place where children could have good, safe fun. So, they filled that need by opening The Playground Fun Center at 5 Event Center Blvd. Children (of all ages!) can play miniature golf, race go-carts, climb a rock wall, play video arcade games or take aim in the batting cages. This is an incredible place where entire families can just hang out together because there is something here for every age. If all of this fun makes you hungry, try the delicious pizza and snacks at the center restaurant. A private party room decorated as a carousel is available for birthday or special parties. Hours are Monday-Thursday and Sunday 11 am- 10 pm, Friday and Saturday until midnight. Call 956-546-8700.

Whether it's a themed party for kids or a corporate grand opening that you need help organizing, Boogedy Bear's Partyland is a "one stop party place" for all of your celebrations. Boogedy Bear's Partyland offers heaven on earth for kids with face painting, an inflatable castle, custom made piñatas and even characters who put on a full show! Full decorating is also available with centerpieces, balloon bouquets and take home baby shower keepsakes. Even if you already have a location, Boogedy Bear's Partyland, 22 Palm Village Shopping Center in Brownsville, offers very competitive prices for professional video, DJ scrvice, catering and event coordinating. Let them help you plan a successful party. Hours are Tuesday-Thursday 10 am-6 pm and Friday-Sunday 10 am-10 pm. For more details about how to customize your event, visit www.boogedybears.com or call 956-541-6920 or toll free 866-391-6920.

DISCOVER EDINBURG

This three time All-America City boasts that it is "Everything Life Should Be!" We think you will agree after visiting this charming Texas city, located just north of McAllen. It is the county seat of Hidalgo County with a population of about 48,500. If you are looking for a relaxed pace of life and the security of a small town—Edinburg is the place. If you need a little more "big-city" excitement, you'll find that, too, in the fast growing metro area. There, you can enjoy the symphony, a concert, or a play. Step right across the border into Mexico and take advantage of the great shopping opportunities! You'll find the people of Edinburg to be friendly and welcoming, fulfilled and enthusiastic, and very proud of their beautiful city. There is truly so much to do and see here, you'll need at least several days.

THE GREAT OUTDOORS

Let the kids drag you to SuperSplash! Adventure, a 35-acre family adventure waterpark featuring the latest, greatest, and coolest water rides in on the world! After the supersoaking slides and wild rides, enjoy live entertainment, souvenir shops and delicious food.

Nature enthusiasts will love El Sal del Rey (Salt of the King), a large salt lake 22 miles north of Edinburg, which was discovered by the Spanish Conquistadors. Salt from the mines was transported to Spain and her colonies and into Mexico. Also, in the spring of 2003, the City of Edinburg opened its World Birding Center. The Scenic Wetland Trails and bird park are set on 40 acres of wetlands adjacent to the 90-acre Edinburg Municipal Park. A nature tourism destination, the site has over one mile of trails and five bird observation platforms. The Edinburg World Birding Center is part of the Lower Coastal Birding Trail and is classified as a premier birding location in South Texas.

There are 13 miles of hike and bike trails available throughout Edinburg, so you can cycle, run or stroll to your heart's content. And if golf is your game, you'll find several championship golf courses to play. The best for last? Texans think so. The Sheriff's Posse Arena, located on S. Highway 281 and West Wisconsin Road, offers Rio Round-Up every Saturday at 6 pm. This includes calf roping, barrel racing and more, and there are two full-scale rodeos held every February. We understand now why people of Edinburg believe that life in their city is . . . "as good as it gets!"

Play ball! The Roadrunners Professional Baseball Park hit a home run with their new state-of-the-art minor league baseball stadium. This professional 4,000 seat stadium has paved the way for Edinburg's entry into the Texas/Louisiana League and will be home of the UTPA Broncs. Amenities include: 10 luxury skyboxes, a large spacious press box, and an awesome electronic scoreboard. For more information, contact the Edinburg Professional Baseball Club at 956-289-8800 or www.roadrunnersbaseball.com.

MUSEUMS AND MEMORIALS

For an educational portrait of Edinburg and Hidalgo County history, be sure to visit the Hidalgo County Historical Museum at 121 E. McIntyre. The fascinating exhibits give a broad overview of the region from prehistoric tribes through Spanish exploration; the Mexican War; Rio Grande steamboat era; the Civil War; border wars; and much more. The museum is located in the 1920 County Jailhouse (complete with a hangman's trap used for public executions.)

For another trip through historic Edinburg, tour the Southern Pacific Railroad Depot at 602 W. University, which is home to the Edinburg Chamber of Commerce Visitor Information Center. Here you will see memorabilia such as a conductor's cap, playing cards, lamps, lanterns, and the original "golden spike" driven on Jan. 11, 1927. Admission is free.

The Hidalgo County Veterans War Memorial is located on the courthouse lawn, and honors Hidalgo individuals killed in action during World War I, World War II, The Korean War, and Vietnam. If you hold your ears just right . . . you might hear the unforgettable rhythm of the South Texas music beat that has so captivated audiences from around the world. The Tejano Walk of Fame was unveiled in 1999, an exciting tribute to Tejano music stars. Five stars were inducted into the walk of fame that first year, and five additional stars will be inducted every year during Hispanic Heritage Month.

VIVA FIESTA EDINBURG!

The last week of February is one of the most exciting times to visit Edinburg because the entire city is having a great big party! You can experience four days of fun and exciting activities for the entire family, including live concerts and carnival rides; parades; rodeos; and lots of great food. You can see Miss Edinburg crowned, participate in a 3-mile run, cheer at a talent show, and of course, eat lots of great food!

For information on Edinburg, call the Edinburg Chamber of Commerce at 800-800-7214 or 956-383-4974 or visit www.edinburg.com.

Edinburg
Fairs Festivals & Fun

February
Fiesta Edinburg
10 K Run

May
LaPlacita/Market Square

December
UTPA Night of Lights

Coffee, Restaurants &
Specialty Foods

As you can imagine by the name, the minute you walk through the door, the wonderful aroma of freshly brewed, gourmet coffee welcomes you—but the name is a little misleading. There is so much more to this classy, cozy place than just coffee.

First of all, it is a family affair. Mike and Deanna Cochran, along with their children, work together to provide their customers with a wonderful atmosphere for coffee and conversation; bridge club luncheons, or romantic dinner dates. The Coffee Zone also features a full Espresso bar, freshly-prepared lunches with homemade pastries, and now a private party room for dinner or special events. For catering information, call 956-381-5462. Coffee Zone is located at 1108 S. McColl Road in Edinburg, and is open Monday-Friday 6:30 am-11 pm, Saturday at 8 am, and Sunday at noon.

ALL TIME SNACKS

The eye catching yellow building at 1321 S. 18th Street in Edinburg resembles a small version of The Alamo. Perfectly located next to the David Soto Cougar's Baseball Stadium and next to a playground and park, All Time Snacks is a favorite for "kids" young and young at heart. Walk up or drive through for delicious fast Mexican food and sweet treats. We tried the corn cups and snow cone—the perfect fast food combination! You will love meeting the owner Sr. Silvestre Villarreal—he loves working with both children and adults. Word of mouth advertising has helped make All Time Snacks very popular. It is open seven days a week, 11 am-8 pm. Call 956-792-0450.

LA JAIBA SHRIMP HOUSE

Contemporary Spanish ballads fill the air and create an ambiance of comfort and fun, but the true star here is the food. La Jaiba Shrimp House, 202 N. 10th Avenue, is known as one of the best seafood restaurants in all of Edinburg. Located right in front of the Courthouse, La Jaiba is a wonderful restaurant that has it all—history, ambiance, and, of course, great seafood!

The beautiful building was once the downtown creamery, and has been architecturally restored to preserve its historical importance. Decorations and framed photographs from Edinburg's early days give the restaurant a warm, comfortable feeling of home. Add pretty tables and chairs, fun music, and the most perfectly cooked shrimp dinner you can imagine, that's what you'll experience at LaJaiba Shrimp House. La Jaiba is open daily 11 am-5 pm. Call 956-316-3468.

FRUIT CUPS & MORE

For a quick snack with a healthy twist, Fruit Cups and More is the place to visit. Offering fruit cups mixed with a variety of fruits and fruit smoothies, whichever you choose will be made fresh with the fruits of your choice. While the Banana-Strawberry fruit smoothie is a best seller, the staff at Fruit Cups and More is willing to try new combinations and make a creation just for you.

Fruit Cups and More, 1226 W. University in Edinburg, is a unique way for people to snack healthy while on the go. Fruit Cups & More is open Monday-Saturday 10:30 am-9:30 pm. For more information, call 956-318-3995.

Cosmetics, Health & Beauty

Let's face it ladies, as we get older, we need a little help looking like the "girl" we once were. Our lips begin to fade from that beautiful natural rose color of the very young, our eyebrows thin and lose their color, and our faces take on a "washed out" appearance. Wouldn't you love to look in the mirror and absolutely love the way you look all day long, without applying lipstick, or "fixing your face?" Molly Norton is the very talented intradermalogists at Cosmetic Alternatives will help you achieve the natural, beautiful look you want using "intradermal permanent cosmetics." Molly has worked in the cosmetic and beauty industry for more than 15 years, and has been associated with pageants such as Miss U.S.A., and Miss Rio Grande Valley.

As a licensed professional Intradermalogist, she offers microdermobrasion, chemical peels, facials, and intradermal pigmentation. This state-of-the-art technique is a method of applying natural pigments into the skin, and is designed to be completely safe. It is used for a variety of enhancements such as permanent eyebrows, eye liner, lip liner and lip color. It can also be used to camouflage scar tissue, stretchmarks and vitiligo.

Molly carries a wonderful line of skincare products called Rejuvi, which were created by Dr. Wade Cheng, Glyquin and Kinerase, and Sebastian foundations and lipsticks.

These "alternative" permanent cosmetics are a relatively inexpensive way to gently turn back the lines of time. The salon is located at 2107 Cornerstone Blvd in Edinburg and is open Monday - Friday 8:30 am - 5:30 pm and Saturday 9 am - 1 pm. Call 956-687-3305.

Gifts & Home Décor

D.G.M. HOME DÉCOR

When your home needs a face-lift, who are you going to call? The experts at D.G.M. Home Décor, that's who! From beautiful bedroom furniture to wild animal print accessories—D.G.M. has it all!

Browse through the store's broad selection of styles and pick out a mirror, lounge or even dining room set that is perfect for your taste. Whether your home is traditional, modern or eclectic, the staff at D.G.M., 302 S. Jackson in Edinburg, will find pieces to compliment your décor.

And, to ensure that your shopping experience is a pleasant one, the staff is there for your every shopping need. From the sale to the home delivery, this family-owned-and-operated business keeps the customer at the forefront. Open Monday-Saturday 10 am-7 pm and Sunday 1-5 pm, D.G.M. awaits your visit. To learn more, call 956-383-6033.

BROADWAY HARDWARE & GIFTS

The staff at the newly-remodeled Broadway Hardware at 511 E. University Street in Edinburg is very excited that the Radio Shack inside the store has garnered the Gold Level Award, and was selected as the Store of the Year! The gift and housewares departments have your favorite items from manufacturers such as Rowenta and Chantal, and a fun collection of high-end gadgets from Rosle. Call 956-383-5603. *(Color picture featured in front section of the book.)*

Golf

Your game will never be more exciting than here at the beautiful Los Lagos Golf Club, 1720 S. Raul Longoria in Edinburg. This incredible award-winning course was designed by the well-respected firm of von Hagge, Smelek and Baril, and is fast becoming the shining star of the golf community in the Rio Grande Valley.

The Par 72 course consists of 11 acres of sparkling lakes, sand, links-style mounding, and just so you'll beware, a killer signature hole (#14!) After conquering the course, check out the 10,000-square-foot clubhouse, and the lighted open-air pavilion with full grill and beverage service. Los Lagos was named a 2002 Top Ten Facility for Overall Customer Loyalty and Satisfaction by the National Golf Foundation. Stop by and find out why. The club is open Monday-Sunday 6 am-7 pm. Visit www.loslagosgolfclub.com or call 956-316-0444.

Weddings

ROYAL CARRIAGES

What little girl hasn't dreamed of being whisked away in a horse-drawn carriage by a dreamy Prince Charming? Norb Nester and his Belgian horses help make these dreams come true throughout the Rio Grande Valley. This Royal Carriage ride, with offices at 3220 W. Sunset Drive in Edinburg, is an experience that will always be a treasured memory. You can choose the Vis-à-vis carriage (French for "face to face"), which holds six adults; or a smaller, cozier carriage for three, perfect for a bride and groom. Each carriage is equipped with a stereo and compact disc player so passengers can set their ideal mood. Open daily from 8 am-10 pm or call 956-289-1650.

DISCOVER HARLINGEN
La Feria

It has been described as a tropical playground, a birder's paradise, a city of festivals, a Mecca for Mexican shoppers, and a safe haven for Winter Texans. Harlingen's magical, magnetic appeal says "Bienvenidos! to her visitors in a warm and wonderful way. Blessed with a climate that even in the winter months, rarely demands long sleeves, Harlingen offers a plethora of exciting, educational, and just plain "fun" activities. The bicultural, tropical flavor of Harlingen beckons everyone outdoors to enjoy shopping, dining, museum browsing, hiking, birding, and even citrus picking. This relatively young town has emerged during its hundred-year life into a vibrant, thriving, community with a casual, friendly, Pan-American setting.

A TEXAS "YOUNG'N"

Only 100 years ago, Anglo settlers began to make their way by wagon, rail, and high-wheeled stagecoach to this land thick with cactus, coyotes, and rattlesnakes. For centuries, it had been home to the Coahuiltecans, until Spanish explorers claimed the region for their country. By 1845, when Texas joined the Union, ferries and steamboats afforded trade all along the Rio Grande, but it was the extension of the railroad that laid the groundwork for this thriving agricultural center.

Visionary Lon C. Hill began clearing land and digging irrigation canals to entice farmers from across the country to the Rio Grande Valley. Because the canals were similar to Holland's waterways, the Dutch name "Harlingen" was chosen for the new town. By 1904, enough residents warranted a post office, and a town center was established. After a two-story hotel was built in 1906, other buildings near the railroad tracks began to spring up, including two general stores, hardware and drug stores, saloons, a blacksmith shop, barbershop, and a Texas Rangers headquarters. With its strategic location in the Valley, Harlingen began to emerge as a thriving trade and transportation hub, and today with its many citrus groves, sugar cane fields, and aloe vera plantations, remains a city with prominence in agriculture.

We found Harlingen to be a truly gracious host on the beautiful southern tip of Texas, and we invite you to trace its rich, cultural history, and enjoy its present day bicultural excitement.

FLOCK TO HARLINGEN AND LAGUNA MADRE

Grab your binoculars, don your most comfy bird-watching duds, and join the migration of birders to one of the nation's top birding destinations. Warm breezes usher in more than 480 species of fowl and 7,000 birders each year to this South Texas birders' paradise. The Laguna Atascosa National Wildlife Refuge, only minutes away from Harlingen, is described as one of the best places to bird in the valley. Visitors cover the 45,187 acres of grasslands to record sightings of birds like sandhill cranes, aplomado falcons, loggerhead strikes, green jays, olive sparrows, and roseate spoonbills. Harlingen also hosts the annual Rio Grande Valley Birding Festival each year in November, which famed birder/priest Father Tom Pincelli helped establish. Don't worry if you don't have a sleeve-length life list (the number of species a birder has spotted in his or her life.) Amateurs and experts alike are welcome to enjoy this wonderful Rio Grande birding paradise.

The magical waters of the beautiful Laguna Madre (translated Mother Lagune,) are located only a short distance from Harlingen, curling south from Corpus Christi, 120 miles to the Rio Grande Delta, stretching on for another 100 miles into Mexico. This salty expanse features a variety of barrier islands, dunes, marshes, sea grass meadows, and waterways offering great fishing and unparalleled beauty. You will almost feel as though you are "walking in the sky," as the crystal blue waters and cloud-free sky seem to meld together in unforgettable visions of coastal beauty.

HARLINGEN "ATRACTIVOS"

Treat your family to homemade ice cream at an old fashioned soda fountain, and see south Texas history come alive through tours of historic Harlingen. The Rio Grande Valley Museum offers an inside look into the city's past with exhibits on ranching, railroads, archaeology, agriculture, and the Civil War. Take home a souvenir treasure—from a piece of old-fashioned rock candy to a cookbook that mixes recipes and history—there's something for everyone.

The Texas Air Museum explores the history of aviation and historic aircraft from World War I and II, Korea, and Vietnam—a favorite for kids of *all* ages, and if you happen to be visiting on the second Saturday of each month from October-March, you'll see special "fly-in" demonstrations.

SHOP 'TILL YOU DROP!

Known as THE antiques capital of the Valley, Harlingen's restored downtown is filled with irresistible crafts, glassware, china, collectibles, jewelry, vintage clothing, furniture, and of course, cowboy boots! It is a charming step back in time to small-town America, where you can celebrate your newly-found treasures over sandwiches or tacos at wonderful cafés and restaurants. However you spend your day in the Jackson Street District, you absolutely must try the delicious *pan dulce*, or sweet bread of the Rio Grande Valley. Mexican bakeries use old and closely guarded secrets in creating traditional favorites such as anillos, molletes, bolillos, and puro e piña. One taste, and your family will be shouting, "Mas, por favor!"

Enjoy the city's parks, nature trails, tennis courts, pools, and picnic shelters, or pack your putter to tackle the challenging golf courses. You'll also want to make time for a trip to Granny Clare's Citrus for tours and tastings. Here you will learn about growing and harvesting citrus, and sample sweet red grapefruit and juicy oranges. Mmmm!

LA FERIA

La Feria "the fair" is a friendly, little community supported by a bounty of crops from the rich land that surrounds it. Once home to Indians in ancient times, this little farming town is populated with hard working people who are some of the friendliest, most genuine Texans you will ever meet.

For more information on Harlingen, call the Harlingen Chamber of Commerce at 956-423-5440 or visit www.harlingen.com.

Harlingen
Fairs Festivals & Fun

January
- Market Days
- Antique Show – Casa de Amistad

February
- Market Days
- Early Aviation Festival
- Wood Carving Show
- Battle Color Ceremony
- Party in the Park

March
- Market Days
- Flower Show
- St. Paddy's Day Celebration (Downtown)

April
- Market Days
- RioFest
- Party in the Park

May
- Market Days
- Blues on the Hill
- Annual Kentucky Derby Day

June
- Market Days
- Blues on the Hill

July
- Market Days
- Blues on the Hill
- Fourth of July Parade & Community Picnic

August
- Market Days

September
- Market Days
- Blues on the Hill

October
- Market Days
- Jackson Street Jubilee
- Annual Fiesta de Amistad
- Shriner's Circus
- Fall Festival

November
- Market Days
- Rio Grande Valley Birding Festival
- Party in the Park

December
- Market Days
- Arroyo Colorado Holiday Lighting
- Christmas Parade
- Piñata Fiesta

Antiques

JACKSON STREET ANTIQUES

Leo and Carmen Garza have been antiquing for more than 17 years and have been customers in every antique store in the Rio Grande Valley. When this extraordinary building at 218 W. Jackson Street in  Harlingen became available, they knew it would be perfect for their enormous collection of antiques—especially with its original tin ceiling, brick walls, and concrete floors. It is pretty incredible—a 7,500 square foot antique mall with more than 50 vendors and consignors who shop the country for unusual and interesting antiques.

At Jackson Street Antiques you'll find European antique furniture, primitives, glassware, collectibles, and beautiful stained glass windows. Presently, they have a group of three mirrors from the Mexican Embassy in Washington D.C. Leo says he has coined the word "eclectors" for their group of eclectic collectors who consistently find the most wonderful items for the store. True antique buffs will think they've died and gone to heaven at this antique mall. Jackson Street Antiques is open Monday-Saturday 10 am-6 pm. Call 956-423-4300.

Antiques and Artisan Emporium

The fascinating mural painted on the side of the three-story building depicts events and happenings in Harlingen, and the inside is filled with antiques and treasures that will delight both novice and veteran collectors. The Antiques and Artisan Emporium at 123 E. Jackson is a shopper's paradise—the kind of place you can easily spend hours browsing. With more than 7,000 square feet of display space and 25 diversified dealers, the Emporium truly has something for everyone. You won't want to miss it!

The building itself was built during the 1920s. For many years, the first floor was Day's Drug Store, and the Palm Hotel rented rooms on the second and third floors. In its early years, Day's Drug Store was a "happening" place to shop and visit. Today, excited shoppers and dealers marvel at the incredible selection of unique antique furniture, polished antique silver and delicate fine china tucked into every corner of the beautiful building. You'll find everything from estate jewelry your great grandma would have wore to church on Sunday, to kitchen gadgets and bowls she might have used to make her famous biscuits. Carnival and Depression Glass, decorative plates, and hard-to-find china patterns are displayed in curios and sideboards along with rare pieces of sterling silver. One of our favorite sections in the Emporium is the collection of fine antique linens—hand towels, bedding, hankies and table linens. They are very pretty and very reasonably priced.

You will love shopping this fun, treasure filled Emporium, and meeting the delightful artisans who are so proud of their collections. It is open Monday-Friday 10 am-5:30 pm and Saturday until 6 pm. For more information, call 956-423-4041.

SIMPLY IRRESISTIBLE

This "simply irresistible" mother-and-daughter decorating team has one of the most loved and respected businesses in Harlingen. The twosome antiqued and collected for years before friends insisted they open a store.

Glenda Williams and GayLynn Foster search high and low for true antiques and unusual gifts for Simply Irresistible, 110 E. Jackson Street. They carry Hearth and Home Cake Candles, old Granite Ware, vintage and old Mexico jewelry, as well as handcrafted jewelry by Resurrecting Rose. GayLynn started hand-painting furniture for her own daughters, and the rest is history. Her Custom Creations are whimsical masterpieces—personal and perfect! You'll love the cozy, down-home atmosphere of this wonderful antique store. Stop by soon! It is open Tuesday-Friday 11:30 am-5 pm and Saturday 11 am-6 pm. Call 956-425-8500.

Art, Artists,
Art Galleries & Framing

HAND OF MAN STAINED GLASS STUDIO

Although Jerrie Howell graduated from college with a degree in Art, her choice of artistic expression took a definite turn when she enrolled in a stained glass class 25 years ago. She opened the first stained glass shop in the Valley in 1977, and today is considered one of the state's premiere glass artists. Hand of Man Studio is located at 1201 W. Jackson Street in Harlingen in the charming building "with the vines on the front."

You'll be amazed at the vast selection of brilliant stained glass art, and at the affordability of it all. Folks from across the continent have commissioned Jerrie to design unique pieces for their homes, offices or churches. We saw a seven foot tall 3-D Lighthouse ready for a restaurant in the Cayman Islands, and a "fish" being shipped to a couple in San Antonio. With know-how, ingenuity, and her handy soldering iron, Jerrie also takes on many items for repair or reconstruction. Stained glass students will find a large variety of supplies, and classes are offered for beginners. Open Monday-Friday 9:30 am-4 pm and Saturday 9:30 am-noon. For more information, call 956-428-4562.

Harlingen Art Forum Gallery

Located on the west side of the downtown historical district, the Harlingen Art Forum Gallery is a unique surprise. It houses an impressive selection of fine art that would rival any large city gallery. Inside the lovely gallery you'll find an excellent collection of oils, pastels, watercolors, collage and sculpture, as well as gift items made of copper, silver, ceramic, and wood. Small collectibles and artists' designed notecards round out the inventory simply wonderfully. All items are affordably priced, and the exhibits change frequently.

The Harlingen Art Forum Gallery is a true teaching gallery with many talented participants. It is the place of choice for art classes and workshops in Harlingen, and it offers an outstanding summer program for children. Located at 305 W. Van Buren, the Harlingen Art Forum Gallery is open Wednesday-Saturday 11 am-4 pm, or by appointment. The Gallery is available at a nominal fee for small private receptions or daytime parties. For more information, call 956-425-4030.

Raised and educated in the Valley, Peggy Allen has been involved in the graphic arts all of her life. Her talent as a framer is evident throughout the House of Frames located at 1206 E. Harrison in Harlingen. With illustrative and studio art experience, Peggy has worked as a television and university graphic artist, in advertising art, and in photography. She uses this experience to create frames that are as impressive as the art they display. Peggy says, "We try very hard to reflect the personality of the art in the framing itself." You'll find a large selection of posters, prints and original pieces of art at the House of Frames. Some of the most unique and popular items in the store are the handmade, one-of-a-kind frame mosaic mirrors. These are made from a sampling of all the types of frame moldings available in the shop. Hours are Monday-Friday 9 am-5 pm and Saturday 10 am-1 pm. Call 956-423-8282.

Camping & RVs

With RV facilities from California to Florida, the Encore RV Resorts offer travelers great places to "Park Your Wheels and Kick Up Your Heels!" More than just a place to hook up your RV and sleep for a few nights, the Harlingen Encore RV Resort offers extensive recreation opportunities and amenities, making it one of the most desirable RV resorts in the area. Many of the large full hook-up sites have lake views, but all have 30/50/100 amp, and telephone service. Campers enjoy a beautiful heated pool, a Jacuzzi, a recreation center, laundromat game rooms, an exercise room, shuffleboard, billiards and much more.

The Resort is a secure vacation haven, as well as a place to meet fun-loving, active people who want the same things out of life as you—adventure, travel, relaxation, fun! Visitors to the Encore RV Resort feel very welcome. Even your pets are treated like family.

Encore Resort-Harlingen is truly a home away from home. The trash is picked up three days a week; the yards are immaculately groomed and tended, and handymen staying onsite will even find a fully-equipped work shop with a vacuum machine attached to every tool. You can also post your mail from a private mailbox on location. There are three large salons and a 13,000 square foot dance hall with parquet floors—perfect for special parties, birthdays, or reunions. The park sponsors many special events designed to bring the campers together such as bingo, pot-luck dinners, card games, tournaments, craft shows, dances and parties. The park is located at 1900 Grace Avenue in Harlingen close to great shopping, exciting restaurants, fabulous fishing spots, golf courses, and Progresso Mexico. You'll find the park open seven days a week, twenty-four hours a day. Visit www.RVontheGO.com online or call 956-428-4137.

Florists,
Gardens & Nurseries

Voted "Best Flower Shop in Cameron County" for five years, Bloomers Flower Shop is a delightful combination of beautiful blooms and wonderful gifts for the home and garden. Visit the charming yellow house at 2001 S. 23rd Street, on the corner of 23rd Street and Ed Carey in Harlingen and be greeted by a friendly, lovable chocolate lab. The talented Pam Fuller, has owned the shop since 1992, but worked for the previous owner for seven years before buying it. Her award-winning design team consists of three Texas Master Florists whose Tropical and European style of flower arranging keeps faithful customers coming back time after time. You'll also find the aromatic Trapp Candles (my favorite) and very unique gifts for the home. Bloomers is open Monday-Friday 8:30 am-5 pm and Saturday 9 am-noon to help you with "every bloomin'thing." Call 800-255-0367, 956-425-2500 or visit www.bloomersharlingen.com.

Grimsell's

Grandfather Frank Grimsell made his way from Minnesota to Harlingen by train during the 1900s as one of the town's earliest pioneers. It was a land of bandits and brush, and not much else. With a pioneering spirit and lots of faith in the future, he purchased a little seed store in 1915 that has remained in the family for almost 90 years! In fact, Grimsell's is in its original location, at 213 W. Monroe Street. The historic building was built in 1904 by Loc C. Hill, the founder of Harlingen, and was usually the center of the town's community business.

Grimsell's is a true Rio Grande tradition. It has always been known as a place to find the largest inventory of roses in the Valley. In fact, its selection of California roses is the largest in Texas! Enjoy the peace and beauty of the lovely rose garden gazebo, and find inspiration for your own garden. Grimsell's also carries the best quality blends of fertilizers, lawn food, insecticides, seeds, and pet foods. Try Grimsell's own product line, Valley Supreme Lawn Food, or try other name brand products.

For your pets, you'll find Science Diet, Eukanuba, Nutro, and Solid Gold Dog and Cat Foods. By the way, you'll probably be greeted by one of their four-legged, furry helpers! Everyone at Grimsell's is so helpful and friendly. Most of the employees have been with the company for more than 20 years, so they are all like family. You'll feel like you've made new friends who really care. That customer service is one of the things that has kept this much-loved business so successful throughout the decades. Hours are Monday-Saturday 8 am - 6 pm and Sunday noon-4 pm. Call 956-423-0370.

Furniture

Coun Y ree Woods

You'll love the clean, fresh-cut wood smell of this special custom furniture store in Harlingen. Owners Michael and Barbara Howland have "carved" a beautiful niche for themselves in the custom furniture business. They build quality, functional based furniture that is designed to give reliable trouble-free use for a lifetime. Whether it is an entertainment center, office furniture, bedroom furniture, children's furniture or other; it is built one piece at a time by hand to the customer's specifications. They build different styles—even special designs of the customer. Only building with strong quality materials, along with finishes that are custom blended and hand-rubbed. At Countree Woods furniture is designed and built to be handed down from generation to generation. Mike and Barbara like to say they are building "tomorrows antiques."

Drop by and meet Mike and Barbara, walk through their woods and discuss your furniture needs to start your own future heirlooms! They are located at 106 W. Jackson Street and the hours are Monday-Friday 10 am-5:30 pm and Saturday 10 am-3 pm. Call 956-421-2113.

Gifts and Home Décor

Scented candles provide a welcoming aroma into this elegant gift shop and tea-room at 1001 E. Tyler Street in Harlingen. Three generations of family and a Calico cat named "Cali" work together in Deena's Gifts and Collectibles, providing a personal touch throughout the store. You'll find an extensive line of Lladro figurines from Spain and collectibles by Harmony Kingdom and Department 56 Villages. Beautiful frames, crystal pieces, crosses, golf decor, baby items, jewelry and Old World ornaments guarantee a wonderful shopping experience. Java lovers will enjoy a coffee corner offering gourmet coffee and delicious pastries, or guests may meet for lunch in the charming Oak Room. Hours are Monday-Saturday 10 am-6 pm. Call 800-807-8732,956-428-1001 or visit www.deenasgifts.com.

When interior designer Gloria Boling was hired to decorate Ruthie Ewers home, a friendship was forged that would change their lives and their careers—as well as the shopping in Harlingen! The two friends opened Glory B's, an incredible, must-see-it-to-believe-it patio furniture and gift shop at 2901 S. 77 Sunshine Strip. Their enthusiasm for life and fun carries over into the ambiance of the store. New customers come in as strangers, but they always leave as friends, promising to return.

New shipments arrive daily from more than 420 vendors with unusual patio furniture and unique gifts for the garden and home. Among the 40,000 gift items, you'll find the popular Lloyd Flanders furniture, Demdaco Angels, and the famous Colonial Candles. The shop itself is charming, and very cleverly decorated. For instance, only an interior decorator such as Gloria would turn unsightly cracks in the floor into beautiful sprigs of painted ivy. Merchandise is arranged in easy-to-shop vignettes featuring angels, roosters, frogs, Americana, hummingbirds, blue and white "everything" and crosses (just to name a few!)

Locals love to hear the clever quips from Gloria and Ruthie each Monday, as they are live over KTEX Radio, sharing amusing information from Glory B's. They offer a frequent buyer card and free gift-wrap, and a promise that no one pays full price! Spend some time with Gloria and Ruthie and let them help you find the perfect item for your patio or home. Also ask about the charming patio available for group meetings. Glory B's is open Monday-Saturday 10 am-6 pm and Thursdays until 8 pm. For more information, visit www.glorybs.net online or call 956-364-2111.

The Red Moon

Gifts, Antiques & Uniques

The Jackson Street District in downtown Harlingen has evolved into quite an amazing place. You will feel the creative energy of the merchants throughout the district! One place that best captures the heart of the Valley is The Red Moon, at 102 W. Jackson Street. Inspired by her artistic husband and three children, Margaret Gonzalez opened the store, which is a vibrant and exciting mix of antiques, art, jewelry, wrought iron and rustic furniture, and unusual gifts for the home.

The store is home to different shop owners and artists, all with one-of-a-kind, hand-made items. The Fisherman's Wife brings in items from Peru—colorful baskets, hand-carved painted gourds, antique mantas and purses, and wonderful religious articles. The popular "Soap Lady" makes soap the old-fashioned way, and sells a variety of scented soaps and bath salts. You'll find fabulous glassware and wonderful kitchen items. Casa Margarita imports wrought iron furniture from Guadalajara—everything from candleholders and garden items to dining tables along with colorful hand woven tablecloths, napkins, and crosses. Also, available at The Red Moon is a wonderful collection of old trains along with train kits and train accessories. You'll also find an amazing compilation of dollhouses and doll furniture. A fantastic section has been developed—called the Tropical Area, which includes Banana Trees to birds. Local artists display their works in oil, acrylic, watercolors, and pen & ink.

The Red Moon is open Monday-Saturday 10:30 am-6:30 pm. Call 956-428-5011.

When Elida Guajardo opened her wonderful gift shop at 11059 Expwy 83, between Robb & Solis roads in La Feria, people came—and they returned bringing friends. Once people find Ele's Gift Shop & Cantera Rancho Alegre, they always return! Ele's is the kind of place that instills fierce loyalty in its customers, because they know they will be able to find the perfect gift or piece for their home as well as personal service.

The building itself is a marvel. The natural stone and hand-carved columns, fountains and balusters outside are beautiful. Elida's husband Silvestre Guajardo built these beautiful stores and you will find the natural Cantera stone in Cantera Rancho Alegre. We loved getting to know Elida and Silvestre as much as we loved shopping in their fine stores.

Once inside, take your time to browse these incredible stores filled with beautiful, and very unusual items. You'll find home accessories, fashion accessories, and children's items, and a wonderful variety of unique treasures. Silvestre and his friends create many of the items. You will absolutely love finding treasures that aren't in department stores—like one-of-a-kind pieces of jewelry, and painted cherubs, and hand-made children's hampers. They also carry a line of luxurious leather furniture not found anywhere in the area, and top-quality leather purses. You are sure to walk away with something wonderful that will be a great memento. Hours are Monday-Friday 9 am-6:30 pm, Saturday until 5 pm, and Sunday 1-3 pm. Call 956-797-9007.

COUNTRY CUPBOARD

Donagayle Gray and Bonnie Keener did not want their store to be a carbon copy gift shop. One step inside Country Cupboard at 113 E. Jackson in Harlingen will assure visitors that it is quite the contrary. They have relied on local and regional craftsmen to supply original merchandise such as hand-poured candles, stitched or painted dolls, and vintage-painted furniture. These accessories, intermingled with antique furniture and linens, are an ingenious blend of old and new. Donagayle and Bonnie explain that their shop is "not a store you can run through quickly ... it's one you have to explore." Hours are Monday-Saturday 10 am-5 pm. Call 956-423-9617.

BROADWAY HARDWARE & GIFTS

Continuing in the tradition her grandfather began back in 1908, Harriette Armacost manages Broadway Hardware Harlingen at 302 W. Jackson Street. She says that her plumbing section is "definitely the best in town," and that the store has a very strong electrical, hardware, and paint department. And, of course you will find excellent customer service! Call 956-423-1111. *(Color picture featured in front section of the book.)*

Hotels & Motels

MARRIOTT COURTYARD

A lush courtyard, a sparkling pool, and a charming gazebo, await your arrival at Harlingen's top-ranked hotel, the Courtyard by Marriott. You will be minutes from the Valley International Airport, and equidistance from all points of interest including Mexico, South Padre Island and the upper valley. Located at the intersection of Hwys 77 and 83, the Courtyard offers express checkout; meeting/banquet facilities; a pool; a restaurant; a safe deposit box; cable television; laundry and valet services; as well as a fitness center; a spa; a heated outdoor pool; a hot tub; and a Jaccuzi. For information and reservations, call 956-412-7800.

"Life's Great at Super 8!" From the friendly, knowledgeable staff to the beautiful double, queen, and king size rooms—it's all super! The Super 8 Motel is located at 1115 South Expwy 77/83 in Harlingen—walking distance to wonderful shopping and dining. The three-story motel has been open since 1995, and was beautifully renovated in 2002. Select from smoking or non-smoking rooms, which include a coffee maker; a refrigerator; a microwave; a hair dryer; and Cable TV. And, in the morning enjoy a complimentary Super Deluxe breakfast of cereal, toast, bagel, assorted pastries, fresh fruit, coffee and juice. Some of the suites include a Jacuzzi, but the entire family will love the large out-door heated pool. A conference room is available for business meetings, with hi-speed Internet and fax service. The staff goes out of its way to make sure you experience that gracious South Texas hospitality. For room and reservations information, call 956-412-8873 or 800-800-8000. *(Color picture featured in front section of the book.)*

RAMADA LIMITED

Comfort is a must for every traveler. Realizing this, the Ramada Limited has made the comfort of its guests number one. Located conveniently near the downtown area, the airport and other shops and eateries, the Ramada Limited, 4401 S. Expwy 83 in Harlingen, offers easy access and extra comfort with its spacious rooms, friendly staff, and continental breakfast each morning. Each room is equipped with a refrigerator, a microwave, cable television and HBO. Handicap accessible rooms, suites and in-room Jacuzzis are also available. Call 956-425-1333 or visit www.ramada.com.

Restaurants

JACK'S PLACE

Owner Jack Knight confidently states that he serves the "perfect Eggs Benedict" and the "most delicious biscuit, sausage and gravy" you've ever eaten. Jack's Place, 101 S. 77 in Harlingen, features tasty home cooking, all-you-can-eat specials, and—we think—cheesecake that's out of this world! The cook's first chore every morning is baking perfect biscuits and beautiful desserts. The day's menu includes spaghetti, chicken 'n dumplings, and sandwiches (Try the chicken-fried ribeye!); the dinner menu includes steak, seafood and pasta. Hours are Monday-Friday 6 am-1:30 pm, Saturday-Sunday 7 am-1:30 pm., and evenings Wednesday-Saturday 4:30-7:30 pm. Call 956-412-0008.

SIMON'S DELI

Look for the black and white tiled wall at 204 E. Jackson Street next to Timeless Treasures, and you've found one of Harlingen's most famous and loved eateries—Simon's Deli. It's a traditional deli with a Southwest style. Family owned and operated for more than 25 years, they know all of their customers on a first-name basis. From the Roast Beef/Mozzarella and Corned Beef/Swiss to the healthy Turkey or Vegetarian, all of the sandwiches are delicious! You'll also love the ice cream and cappuccino! Simon's prepares box lunches, too, for one to 1,000 and can cater your next special event. Open Monday-Friday 9 am-4 pm, Saturday 11 am-3 pm. Call 956-428-4117.

Salons & Spas

...A DISTINCTIVE EXPERIENCE

"Everyone—regardless of income level—deserves to be pampered!" This philosophy, and the personal attention each customer receives, has made Orchids Day Spa & Salon a favorite place in Harlingen. Centrally located at 1600 W. Tyler, Suite A, Orchids Day Spa & Salon is beautifully decorated to provide an elegant, soothing atmosphere. Owner Lisa Vento is very proud of two products featured at Orchids—the Pevonia Skin Care Products for the face, body, and feet, (which are botanical in nature), and the Aquage Hair Care Products made from sea vegetation and sea minerals. You will also find a wonderful line of aromatherapy gift candles. Whether you need a facial, manicure, pedicure, or a deep tissue massage, you will love being pampered at Orchids Day Spa & Salon. Hours are Monday 10 am-6 pm, Tuesday-Thursday 9 am-6 pm, and Friday 10 am-5 pm. Call 956-425-2122.

Skin Care Treatments

Pampering yourself is what a vacation or even a day off is all about, and no one understands that better than the staff at Bella Kara. For more than 15 years, people have been depending on Bella Kara for their skin care and beauty needs, and it's easy to see why.

The professionals at Bella Kara believe that "the appearance of a person's skin is a reflection of the overall health of that person," and they make sure each person walks out her healthiest. To help ensure this, Bella Kara has specially-formulated products and treatments to care for acne, blemishes, dehydration and even wrinkles, just to name a few.

While your skin is getting pampered, so will you. Indulge in a SlenderQuest wrap and let the inches come off, regaining your youthful, tight skin in just two hours. The SlenderQuest body wrap is a European remedy for compressing fatty tissues, including cellulite, helping to "tone the underlying muscles." Or, just soak away your troubles in a hydrotherapy bath or a Russian steam bath.

Make sure to browse through the many skin and body products at Bella Kara when you visit. Bella Kara offers it all—from face lotion and firming creams, to New Life (a dietary supplement that helps with energy, brain activity and weight loss).

Whether it's a massage, a facial, a haircut and color, a manicure or a pedicure you're in need of, Bella Kara is the place to go. Bella Kara is much more then just a day spa and hair salon—it's pampering that's good for the body and soul.

Easy to find, this beautiful salon is just off of Tyler Street in the downtown area, 1114 E. Tyler Street in Harlingen. Open Monday through Saturday, 10 am-7 pm, appointments at other times may be made by phone. Call 956-440-8888.

Specialty Shops,
Gourmet & Specialty Foods

JUDY'S STITCHERY NOOK

Judy Brady laughingly says that most every needle-point devotee has spoken the words: "just one more stitch, then I will clean the house (or cook dinner; or iron; or . . .") Judy was first introduced to needlepoint by her maternal grandmother at the age of 16 and years later, Judy's love for needlepoint resulted in Judy's Stitchery Nook at 1046 N. 77 Sunshine Strip #2 in Harlingen. Since it's beginnings in 1989, the shop has grown to overflowing with an ever-changing inventory of exciting needleart merchandise. You'll find large selections of specialty fabrics, threads, accessories, and needlepoint canvases. Although Judy's first priority is providing the finest quality needleart supplies, her friendly, personalized service has been the backdrop to her success. Classes are available for all ages and skill levels. Open Monday-Friday 10 am-5:30 pm and Saturday 10 am-4:30 pm. Call 956-421-2654.

SERENDIPITY OF THE VALLEY

If you're looking for that ideal gift for a friend or business customer, Serendipity of the Valley in San Benito has what you need. Whether it's the Gourmet Jelly, the mouthwatering Salsa, or the large variety of spices, all are homemade with the freshest of Texas' ingredients. Look for Christine or Dennis Caffey at one of the many trade shows they attend each year, and sample some of their unique South Texas creations. Gift packs can be shipped anywhere in the United States. If you have a hard time making it to a trade show, call 800-420-8409 or don't worry because you can see Serendipity's full-line of products at www.serendipityofthevalley.com.

QUILT & FABRIC SHOP

Take a 50-year-old run down bar, paint it, fix it up, and turn it into a pretty quilt shop! Betty and Robert Veale did just that at 2815 S. 77 Sunshine Strip in Harlingen—now the Picket Fence Quilt & Fabric Shop. Ladies now belly up to the bar with their newest quilt creations, and the "regulars" meet to eat, quilt, and learn. Beautifully stitched quilts decorate the walls, and the rooms are filled with bolts of wonderful fabric, a large selection of quilting accessories, books, magazines, and sewing machines. Betty says she loves that people no longer sew because they need to; they sew for fun. Every Tuesday is "Hang Out Day," when Picket Fence welcomes customers to bring in and work on their latest project. Classes are held in quilting, old-fashioned appliqué, block making, and bargello. Store hours are Monday-Saturday 10 am-5 pm, until 8 pm on Wednesday. Call 956-412-2668.

WILD BIRD CENTER

After 20 years as an engineer in manufacturing and special education, Bob and Arlene Stelzer have finally found their "niche!" The Wild Bird Center at 509 S. Expwy 83, Suite H-8, in Harlingen, is a fun and very interesting specialty store that caters to the casual backyard birder as well and avid field birder.

Field birders will find optics, field guides, and outfitting gear. Backyard birders will love the selection of various feeders, birdbaths, and special blends of seed guaranteed to attract many species to one's backyard. You'll also find beautiful statues, and stepping-stones, whimsical lawn art, and native Valley plants to enhance your yard or garden. The Wild Bird Center is a place for birders to meet and share their knowledge and experiences. You don't need to be an avid birder to enjoy this amazing store. One of the most popular items sold at the Wild Bird Center is the Lil'Flickers candle. Arlene makes these highly aromatic and long-burning candles. Butter Rum is rapidly becoming the most famous scent, as customers throughout the United States call in their orders. Be sure to visit this unique store, and say hello to "Church" the store cat. A cat in a bird store?! Wild Bird Center is open Monday-Saturday 10 am-6 pm. Call 956-428-2211.

DISCOVER McALLEN
Hidalgo / Alamo City / Pharr / Reynosa

It was shortly after the turn of the century that adventurous farmers began to settle the fertile Rio Grande Valley. With the help of irrigation, they began producing beautiful crops of sugar cane and citrus, and were said to "make the desert bloom." But, the biggest boom to the Valley's growth was the arrival of the railroad. That's when the town of McAllen was born. The town was named for Scottish-born Army Captain John McAllen, a Matamoros businessman who bought 80,000 acres of land there after the Civil War, and who was instrumental in bringing the rail to this part of the Valley.

In just a century, McAllen has emerged as the financial center of the Valley with a booming retail and wholesale industry. The tourist industry, petroleum business, international trade and agribusiness make up the city's economy—drawing many to its city limits. And, its warm, balmy climate and relaxed tropical setting make it a wonderful place for "Winter Texans." In addition, McAllen offers many cultural, business, and educational opportunities for its citizens.

McAllen also boasts an excellent arts and science museum and a full calendar of cultural events. And, shoppers looking for bargains will love the city's location. Because it is just eight miles from its Mexican "sister city" of Reynosa, McAllen is a favorite with families looking for a chance to shop at the traditional "mercado." Hotels offer van service to the International Bridge, or you may park your car for the day on the Texas side for just a few dollars.

Into birding? You're in luck. Only 16 miles southeast of the city, birders will find the Santa Ana National Wildlife Refuge, where many rare species are sighted each year, and interpretive tram rides are available during the winter months.

CITY ATTRACTIONS

Among the many fascinating family attractions are the McAllen International Museum of Art and Science, the McAllen Railroad Depot, and the McAllen War Memorial. Providing a look back to the city's early days, the International Museum of Art and Science, at 1900 Nolana, offers both permanent and changing displays. You'll find a wonderful combination of art, science and folk art collections. Call 956-682-1564 for times. Located one block south of Business Hwy 83 on Bicentennial Blvd, the Railroad Depot is now a modern office building, whose exterior has been restored to reflect its original Spanish Colonial appearance. If you're into architecture, bring your camera. Next door, the War Memorial houses memorials to the McAllen War Dead, and is marked as the campsite of "The Fighting 69th" during the border bandit days.

Sports enthusiasts will certainly stay busy enjoying the many challenging golf courses, tennis courts, swimming pools, bowling and miniature golf centers. Also, the McAllen Chamber of Commerce hosts many elaborate holiday celebrations, so plan a trip over a holiday and take advantage of the fun!

BIRDERS' PARADISE

Whether you are a seasoned birder or just "in training," you will love the Texas Tropics Nature Festival, which takes place in McAllen each spring. More than 490 bird species and 240-plus butterfly species have been sighted. Birding spots include Santa Ana National Wildlife Refuge, Bentsen State Park, Quinta Mazatlan, McAllen Bird Pond, and McAllen Nature Center. Let the birding begin!

DO SI DO

Grab your partner, Partner, because McAllen is known as "The Square Dance Capital of the World!" The city hosts so many square dances that the Chamber of Commerce publishes an annual directory for its dances and classes. Every year, square dancers from across the country gather for the Texas Square Dance Jamboree. For information on the date and time, contact the Chamber at 956-682-2871. Beginner dancers will enjoy the "World's Largest Beginners' Square Dance Class," which meets every Monday morning in January at the convention center.

SHOP 'TIL YOU DROP!

International travelers come from many miles to shop McAllen. We have identified the tucked-away, off-the-beaten-path shops and would like to introduce you to all of the great places for your "Lady's Day Out." Grab a delicious lunch or dinner at one of the many fine eateries, and then get ready for a day of incredible shopping. In fact, take a day or *two* to discover all of the wonderfully unique treasures that McAllen has to offer! And remember, wear comfy shoes. We're talking serious shopping!

HIDALGO

Although you might think of Hidalgo as a small quiet town on the United States border with Mexico, it is also a city rich in history, culture, and tradition, and one of Texas' oldest cities. Established in 1749 as "Mission San Joaquin Del Monte," the settlement was later named Edinburgh and then Hidalgo. With the river so close, a pumphouse was built in 1909, and is today a restored and recorded historic site and museum. The Pumphouse offers visitors exhibits that demonstrate how steam powered irrigation pumps transformed the Valley into the agricultural center for the nation. For tour information, call 956-843-8686.

Did you know that you will find the world's largest Killer Bee right on the lawn of the Hidalgo Library? It was built as a parade float to showcase the killer bees that first entered the United States through Hidalgo in 1990.

The city is growing and changing at a rapid pace. There are parks, playgrounds, a new events center, a new ice hockey team, and a multitude of business opportunities related to international trade. Historic buildings such as the Hidalgo Courthouse and Jail, the Old Post Office, and the Rodriguez Store are fascinating attractions for visitors, and the town has several festivals and celebrations. In fact, the largest and oldest heritage music festival in South

Texas—BorderFest—began in 1977, and is held the first weekend in March. For more information on Hidalgo's attractions and festivals, contact the Hidalgo Chamber of Commerce at 956-843-2734. Visit www.hidalgotexas.com online to see a wonderful overview of the city's many exciting attractions.

ALAMO CITY

This agricultural town had several unusual names including "Ebenezer" before the citizens settled on the current name, Alamo. (Much better!) It is the site of the popular Santa Ana Wildlife Refuge, which is located south of the town on U.S. 281. The refuge boasts more species of birds than any other spot in the United States. It's no wonder why it attracts birders from all over the world. Three trails totaling 12 miles stop at three man made lakes and bird-watching blinds. You won't want to miss any of it! Tram tours are available on seasonal schedules, and the center is open from dawn till dusk.

PHARR

It's a Pharr better way . . . this "Hub City" of the Valley is a city on the rise, with fun events and interesting places to visit. Located at the very tip of Texas, Pharr is only seven miles from enchanting Mexico, and celebrates the best of both cultures. Saltwater sportsmen have access to the Gulf of Mexico, and the country is filled with deer, javelina, quail, and whitewing dove. The Pharr-Reynosa International Bridge, which provides a direct link to Mexico and the Maquila Plants, is a major reason for the burst of industry that the city is experiencing. Pharr also boasts of ocelot, jaguarondi, wild turkey and other unique birds and animals that are able to travel freely under the bridge between the wetlands on both sides of the river.

Thousands of people pilgrimage every week to the beautiful "Virgin de San Juan del Valle Shrine," and the annual Fine Arts Show and Sale draws artists from the United States, Canada and Mexico. One of the most exciting events each year is the "Taste of the Valley," which is an event to highlight the variety of restaurants in Pharr and the Valley.

REYNOSA

The colorful town of Reynosa which is McAllen's "sister city" on the Mexican side of the border, was founded in the mid 1700s by Spaniard Don Jose De Escandon. There are 11 current border crossings in the Rio Grande Valley, one of them being the Pharr/Reynosa crossing. This bridge has the longest border crossing in the world at 3.2 miles. The street serpentining down off the bridge leads directly into La Zona Rosa, "the pink zone," which is a concentration of gift shops, restaurants, and discos. Reynosa has recently become a shopper's paradise, so get ready for fun! It is a great little place to spend a few hours bargain hunting, or simply relaxing with a cool beverage.

For more information on McAllen, call the McAllen Chamber of Commerce at 956-682-2871 or visit www.mcallencvb.com.

For more information on Hidalgo, call the Hidalgo Chamber of Commerce at 956-843-2734 or visit www.hidalgotexas.com.

For more information on Alamo City, call the Alamo City Chamber of Commerce at 956-787-2117 or visit www.alamochamber.com.

For more information on Pharr, call the Pharr Chamber of Commerce at 956-787-1481 or visit www.visitpharr.com.

McAllen / Hidalgo / Pharr
Fairs Festivals & Fun

January
Winter Stage Entertainment
Series
Winter Texan Appreciation Day
McAllen International Travel
Show
McAllen Street Market

February
Winter Stage Entertainment
Series
Winter Texan Talent Show
"Spring Classic" Benefit Fine
Arts Show and Sale
Heart of the Valley Health Fair
Square Dance Jamboree
McAllen Street Market

March
Texas Tropics Nature Festival
Hidalgo BorderFest
McAllen Street Market
International Food Festival

April
RGV Homeshow
Taste of the Valley

May
International Food Festival
Mayor' Prayer Breakfast
(Pharr)

June
Mayor's Challenge Golf
Tournament (Pharr)

July
McAllen's Annual Fourth of
July Parade & Fireworks
Fajita Cookoff

August
Hispanic Music Fan Fest
Pharr Night Out

October
Wild Walk Outdoor Adventure
Pharr Phall Phestival

November
McAllen Health Fair
Veteran's Day Parade &
Celebration
McAllen International
Friendship Run

December
All Valley Winter Fruit and
Vegetable Show
Texas' Largest 5K Judged
Race Walk
Candlelight Posada
Hidalgo Festival of Lights
Dias Festivos

City of Hidalgo

Hidalgo Pumphouse
Heritage & Discovery Park

Although you might think of Hidalgo as a small quiet town on the United States border with Mexico, it is also a city rich in history, culture, and tradition, and one of Texas' oldest cities. Established in 1749 as "Mission San Joaquin Del Monte," the settlement was later named Edinburgh and then Hidalgo. With the river so close, a pumphouse was built in 1909, and is today a restored and recorded historic site and museum. The Pumphouse offers visitors exhibits that demonstrate how steam powered irrigation pumps transformed the Valley into the agricultural center for the nation. For tour information, call 956-843-8686.

Did you know that you will find the world's largest Killer Bee right on the lawn of the Hidalgo Library? It was built as a parade float to showcase the killer bees that first entered the United States through Hidalgo in 1990.

The city is growing and changing at a rapid pace. There are parks, playgrounds, a new events center, a new ice hockey team, and a multitude of business opportunities related to international trade. Historic buildings such as the Hidalgo Courthouse and Jail, the Old Post Office, and the Rodriguez Store are fascinating attractions for visitors, and the town has several festivals and celebrations. In fact, the largest and oldest heritage music festival in South Texas—BorderFest—began in 1977, and is held the first weekend in March. For more information on Hidalgo's attractions and festivals, contact the Hidalgo Chamber of Commerce at 956-843-2734. Visit www.hidalgotexas.com online to see a wonderful overview of the city's many exciting attractions.

Antiques

 Eloquently put by some of its biggest fans, Vida is described as being in the business of "raising border living to an art." As you walk into Vida, the aroma of scented candles and the sound of the Spanish guitar music playing softly in the background greet you, creating the perfect setting for this "antique meets folk art shop." Old and new furniture from Mexico, India and England create a quirky mix with lamps, accessories and fun floral arrangements.

Come in for a taste of "old Mexican bazaar, gift store and upscale junk shop." Housed in a beautifully decorated, 1930s stucco building, Vida, 133 W. Business 83 in McAllen, offers its customers a "unique South Texas look." Owners Erren Seale and Fernando Rivera describe it as "Border Chic." Open Tuesday-Saturday 10 am-6 pm. For more information, call 956-686-6086.

SHABBY CHICKS

We loved the name—and you'll love everything inside this adorable antique and gift shop at 8620 N. 10th Street in McAllen. The building was once a gas station, which was built during the 1940s. Now, decorative sheets cover the entire ceiling, and unique treasures fill the rooms. Unlike many antique stores decorated in "shabby chic," this one is refreshingly uncluttered and simple. In fact, it is decorated much as you would furnish your own house, and that makes every visitor feel immediately "at home." Shabby Chicks was the long time dream come true for Mary Garza, who for many years collected and decorated as a hobby. Along with her manager Rosa Delgado, the "chicks" will help you find the perfect antiques or accessories for your home. In addition to furniture and collectibles, she also offers furniture restoration. The shop is open Monday-Saturday 10 am-6 pm. Call 956-686-5044.

Bed & Breakfasts, Cabins, Cottages & Inns

Alamo Inn

The historic Alamo Inn is uniquely set in the heart of the charming Rio Grande Valley. With the option of Bed and Breakfast or accommodations without breakfast, each historic suite has a different feel and atmosphere.

The South Padre Island studio suite sets the mood for relaxation with its beach décor and lighthouse theme, while the Johnson Suite offers roomier accommodations and a taste of the Old West with its pioneer theme.

The Edinburgh Suite is a step back in time with a touch of Victorian style, and you can experience the Deep South in the Pancho Villa Suite. Whichever you pick, satisfaction is guaranteed with comfortable suites furnished with family antiques.

If you decide to take advantage of the beautiful surrounding area, set off for a day of bird and butterfly watching in the nicest birding area in North America. Close by is the famous Santa Ana National Wildlife Refuge. Alamo Inn offers free maps and brochures and has an extensive birding and nature shop. Or treat yourself to shopping and dining in the culturally diverse Rio Grande Valley. Old Mexico is just 20 minutes from Alamo Inn for wonderful dining and shopping just across the border, easy and conveniently close.

The inn is a perfect location in safe, clean, green Alamo to use as your base from which to explore the valley. It will be expanding too, adding charming garden suites to its historic suites. And for those who are adventurous, the inn offers guided personal birding tours and canoe birding trips on the Rio Grande.

For more information visit www.alamoinnsuites.com or call 956-782-9912.

GUEST RANCH

Located in the lower Rio Grande Valley just north of McAllen, the Texan Guest Ranch is nestled among 20 acres of native trees, whispering palms and brilliant flowering bougainvillea. The Guest ranch is a veritable paradise for traveling business people, maquiladora specialists, vacationers and Winter Texan regulars. The spacious apartments and suites are the perfect blend between a motel and an apartment, offering the best of both, including modern kitchens, cable TV, phone, Hi-speed internet service, maid service, laundry and a workout facility. It's a true home away from home.

A charming glassed-in lobby is the perfect place to start your day with a complimentary coffee and the melodious sounds of many native songbirds. The entire grounds are beautifully land-scaped to attract humming birds and butterflies, and the walking trails offer a peaceful escape from a busy world. A center tropical pool area features a heated pool, Jacuzzi, Gazebo, and a Swing House—all for the private enjoyment of their guests.

The ranch has been receiving guests for more than 75 years and offers that "historic" feeling with the updated comfort for true Southern hospitality. Family-owned-and-operated, The Texan Guest Ranch offers apartments and suites rented by the week or the month. The Texan Guest Ranch specializes in extended stay accom-modations with corporate rates available. The family and staff invite you to come and enjoy the magic of the Texas Guest Ranch during your next visit to South Texas. For more information or reservations, call 956-686-5425 or visit www.texasguestranch.com.

Children's Shops
& Art Galleries

CHILDREN'S CLOTHES

If you recognize the brand names Sweet Potatoes, Two Turtles, Petite Bateau, Mulberri Bush, or Giggle Moon, you probably have a new-born, infant, or toddler, and know that these are top-of-the-line names in children's clothing. You'll find all of these and much more at the adorable children's shop, Sweet "P", at 5000 N. 23rd Street, Suite H in McAllen.

The whole shop feels like a playroom, and the staff is wonderful at entertaining the children while moms shop. Expectant mothers are invited to come in and set up a shower gift registry. You'll love browsing through all of the adorable baby gifts and nursery items. Be sure to ask about one of Sweet "P's" newest, and most popular lines, Anne Geddes. Owner Debbie Sakulenzki is friendly and helpful and makes shopping a delightful experience. Store hours are 10 am-6 pm Monday-Saturday. Call 956-631-8400.

SYLVAN
LEARNING CENTER®

The new Sylvan Learning Center, 901 Dove Ave. in McAllen, joins a family of almost 900 centers across North America—all helping children develop a love of learning that pays dividends for a lifetime. The "Sylvan Advantage" offers individual attention, personalized lesson plans, highly trained and certified teachers. There are no two children alike, some struggle, while others are not challenged enough. At Sylvan they will learn to feel better about themselves, and feel better about school. You'll see the change in their eyes, and in their attitude, but most of all, you'll see it in the big smiles on their faces. The smile on a child's face and the pride in a parent's eyes reflect those moments when the whole family realizes what the folks at Sylvan have known all along—learning feels good! Hours are Monday-Thursday 8 am-8 pm, Friday 8 am-6 pm and Saturday 9 am-1 pm. Visit www.educate.com online or call 956-682-9800.

ART CONNECTION

The art displayed in this very unique studio will bring tears to your eyes, as you realize that it is all the work of children—children who have learned to express themselves with color and texture, and who paint a world through innocent eyes. Art Connection at 5401 N. 10th Street, #109-B in McAllen is the creation of Lucia de la Garza and Mily Villegas, who were inspired by similar studios popular in Mexico. Classes are held from Monday thru Saturday for children only, where they learn the tools for painting, and the techniques needed to create their masterpieces. Art Connection is LIFE! For information on class schedules, call 956-664-8278 or 956-330-4335.

Florists, Gardens & Landscaping

To Jacque Hull, her floral business is a calling. She says that being in the floral business affords her the opportunity to share her Christian love with so many people at some of the most important moments in their lives. People buy flowers for incredibly happy times, like weddings and anniversaries, but they also want the comfort of flowers in times of sadness.

Jacque and her wonderful staff at Jac-Lin's Florist can meet your needs no matter what the occasion! The sweet smelling rooms are filled with beautiful flowers, wreaths, and lots of happy people. Weddings are an important part of Jacque's business, and her exquisite gift baskets are the talk of the town. The head floral designer is a true artist with flowers, creating arrangements that garner praise at every event. Located at 722 N. Main Street in McAllen, and is open Monday-Friday 8 am-6 pm and Saturday 9 am-5 pm. Call 956-686-5252.

FLAMINGO POOLS

Grab your float and head outside to enjoy the crystal, cool, waters of your swimming pool. If you live anywhere in the Rio Grande Valley, a backyard swimming pool is a "must!" If you don't have one, Dennis Gomez and the belly-flopping team at Flamingo Pools can have one built in your back-yard within a few weeks. Visit the Flamingo Pools showroom at 721 W. Dove Street in McAllen for ideas that would best suit your family and landscape. You will be surprised at the many different styles and shapes—no cookie-cutter pools here. And, easy payment plans allow any family to enjoy this great source of entertainment. Dennis has one of the few pool companies that do custom work for both in-ground and aboveground pools. The showroom is open Monday-Friday 8 am-7 pm, Saturday until 5 pm and Sunday 10 am-3 pm. For more information visit www.flamingo-pools.com or call 956-618-0101.

Furniture

HERITAGE HOME ACCENTS

Because the front door is the first impression of your home, it is important to have one that makes a beautiful statement. If your door is from Heritage Home Accents at 705 East U.S. Business Hwy 83 in Pharr, you can be assured that it will be a one-of-a-kind piece of art. They are all hand-made according to the customer's design, usually out of beautiful mesquite wood.

Owner Jason Hatton began working with mesquite wood to build fine furniture for his own home. He feels that the wood's beautiful grain creates interesting design possibilities in each piece of art. What started as a hobby has grown into a very successful custom door and accessory business, and now he furnishes his mesquite doors to customers throughout Texas. Heritage Home Accents is open Monday-Friday 8 am-5 pm. For more information visit www.heritagehomeaccents.com or call 956-227-6211.

HACIENDA SAN MIGUEL

Alejandro and Eugenia Alvarez are life-long entrepreneurs who have combined their love for travel, shopping, and people into a wonderful furniture and home décor business. Hacienda San Miguel, at 1414 N. 10th Street in McAllen, offers one of the largest selections of Talavera pottery, hand-painted items, and Equipales (Mexican leather chairs) north of the border. The Alvarez family loves traveling in search of the very unique and unusual, knowing that their clientele appreciates their effort. The Equipales they offer are wonderful pieces similar to those seen in magazines such as "Santa Fe Style," and their selection of crosses will please even the most particular collector.

Alejandro and Eugenia have lived in the Valley since 1956 and consider themselves "natives." Their large and friendly family is very involved in helping run the business, so it is quite a family affair. Be sure to look for the Hacienda San Miguel booth at "Dias Festios" every year. Hours are Monday 10:30 am to 6 pm and Tuesday-Saturday 10 am to 6 pm. Call 956-683-9335.

Beautiful, soothing music creates a peaceful atmosphere, complimenting the unusual and wonderful mix of decorating possibilities at Celina's Interiors, 720 Nolana Street in McAllen. Here you will experience a place that brings together furniture, unique items, and artwork from India, Indonesia, Latin America, Asia, Africa and Mexico. These creations are made by artists who put a touch of "magic" into creating works of great quality. Celina's Interiors also offers professional decorators to assist you in choosing fine antiques, period furniture, tables, lamps, mirrors and incredible accessories that will give any space a one-of-a-kind appearance.

The unique items at Celina's fit together like old friends. You'll find pieces made from natural stone, wood, and custom iron—combinations that display art, shapes and color in very different dimensions.

Celina Ahlman has created an elegant showroom, filled with beautiful pieces from the past and paired with very unique accessories that dramatically inspire the imagination. Hand-carved four-poster beds are draped in sheer fabrics; Moroccan tables hold floral masterpieces; and custom-made bedding and draperies finish the room in style. Whether you are looking for a very dramatic piece for a special room, or just a little something for a tabletop, you'll love the uniqueness of everything in this store. You'll find heirlooms to enjoy for generations! For your convenience, shipping options are available upon request. Store hours are Monday-Saturday 10 am-6 pm. Please visit online at www.celinasinteriors.com or call 956-668-0004 or 956-668-1775. *(Color picture featured in front section of the book.)*

Gifts & Home Décor

Sollet
UNIQUE GIFTS & CRAFTS

When Raquel Tello told her parents she was thinking of opening her own gift shop, she was a bit hesitant—since she was only 22. What happened? They reacted the way they always had…with support and encouragement. So with that, Sollet Unique Gifts & Crafts, 5401 N. 10th Street, #109-C in McAllen was created. Sollet

started from Raquel's joy of creating a variety of hand-painted items, from small wooden keepsake boxes to custom painted furniture. She literally loses track of time while painting. The keepsakes can be ordered in large quantities for special occasions or you can choose from a variety of previously painted pieces. There is also an array of authentic pieces from Central and South America. Open Monday-Saturday 11 am-7 pm. Visit www.luvyamore.com or call 956-686-3410.

Casa Antigua, 1631 N. 10th Street in McAllen, offers an exclusive line of hand-crafted metal furniture and accessories designed by owner Rosario Gonzalez. There are more than 450 unique items, from metal chargers and lamps to intricate fireplace screens and barstools—many of these featured in upscale catalogs. You'll find beautiful hand-crafted pieces from India, Indonesia, Pakistan, Morocco, and Mexico. Hours are Monday-Saturday 10 am-6 pm. For more information, call 956-664-2999.

Since 1988, Barn White has grown to become one of McAllen's most prestigious gift shops located at 4317 N. 10th Street. Enjoy shopping in a unique 50 year-old-home, which has been transformed into a "white barn" framed in baby blue and white clouds. You can't miss it! Owners Sadie Friedrichs and her two daughters, Leslie Ewers and Page Moore, travel New York, Atlanta, and Dallas several times each year to bring their vision of fine gifts, jewelry and home décor to the Valley.

There are literally hundreds of gift lines. You will find the most amazing selection of fine gifts for the home, including exquisite tabletop pieces, fine china and crystal. It's no wonder Barn White's bridal—and baby—registry are the most popular in town.

Special baby clothing, pampering bath products from Lady Primrose, cotton pajamas, signature scented candles, and one-of-a-kind furniture pieces are found dotted throughout and change with the seasons. Barn White is always filled with wonderful ideas for you to bring into your home and it is the valley's only Christopher Radko *Rising Star Store*, so ornaments can be found year round! In fact, Christopher Radko has approved a specially-designed, limited ornament made exclusively for Barn White's customers. Hours are Monday-Saturday 9:30 am-6 pm. The coffee is always on.

For more information, visit www.barnwhite.com or call 956-687-7637. Remember…Barn White Delights!

OH KAY'S!

Kay Jancik's early involvement in the antique business resulted in a discerning eye for quality, craftsmanship, and style, and gave her the expertise to blend trendy with old. The ultimate result? Something she calls, "Tradition with a Twist," and you are going to love it! This one-of-a-kind upscale specialty shop at 4300 N. 10th Street in McAllen features MacKenzie-Childs from New York, Mary Rose Young from England, R Wood from Georgia, Luna Garcia and B Ware from California, and the ever-popular Jon Hart luggage from Texas. Favorite seasonal accessories include Dept. 56 and Christmas Villages, which are available year round to compliment your unique or traditional holiday decorating styles. There is so much to see!

A complete bridal registry includes the timeless classics such as Waterford, Wedgwood, and Reed & Barton, as well as uncommon accessories with a twist of the unexpected. Kay is proud to feature the MacKenzie-Childs' line—a rare collection of reinvented Majolica, mouth-blown glassware, hand-made and hand-painted furniture and functional enamelware. It is a blend of hours of artistry with attention to detail, resulting in true heirloom pieces.

Oh Kay's offers personal shopping service and special attention in the store or over the phone. Store hours are Monday-Saturday 10 am-6 pm. Call 956-686-1264.

BROADWAY
Hardware & Gifts

When Tony and Willie Aguirre were given the opportunity to purchase Broadway Hardware, they instinctively knew it would be a brilliant business decision—they were right. They created a winning combination—between this 50-year-old hardware icon and their already successful McAllen Bolt & Screw. Because Broadway Hardware was known throughout the United States and Mexico, it allowed them to serve both their commercial and residential customers with the greatest possible selection of products and award winning service.

Broadway Hardware was the long time dream of Jack Whetsel, original owner and a former McAllen Mayor. Through the years, he built this enormously successful business by finding the best products and providing the best service. He is happy the Aguirres have continued the tradition in customer care.

Shoppers love the many "stores within the store" at Broadway Hardware, touting it as the ultimate shopping experience. It is one of the few places in the Valley where you can still find gas powered model airplanes. And, you will find replacement cords and parts for every imaginable appliance, as well as an impressive selection of kitchen, sporting, and agricultural knives.

This hardware store is not for "guys only." Brides and grooms love the bridal registry for unusual home items, and birding enthu-

siasts use the store as a headquarters for birding equipment such as binoculars and scopes.

There are two locations to serve you, S. 10th & Jackson Street, call 956-687-6129; and N. 10th and Dove Street, call 956-682-2020. *(Color picture featured in front section of the book.)*

GIFT GODDESS

The "Gift Goddess of the Rio Grande Valley," also known as Julie Morgan, credits the success of her eclectic, funky, and totally unique gift shop to the fact that she had no formal retail experience. With no hard and fast rules to follow, she painted fabulous  murals on the walls, hung unusual shelving and filled the store with things you can't usually find in the Valley. You'll find a collection of art, jewelry and very trendy accessories.

One of the store's biggest assets is Julie herself. She hand-paints items, along with offering art lessons. Julie also contracts to paint murals for homes and offices, or children's portraits, and has built quite a reputation in McAllen and surrounding areas.

The Gift Goddess is located at 833 W. Dove Avenue, and is open Monday-Saturday 10:30 am-8 pm. For more information, call 956-618-2600.

VELDANY'S GIFTS

 The best hidden treasures in town…You won't be able to pass it by. The brightly-painted house and the wonderful wrought iron furniture and garden ornaments will beckon you inside Veldany's Gifts. Owner Mary Perez found the charming 100-year-old-home at 4219 W. Hwy 83 in McAllen to be the perfect backdrop for her hand-crafted wrought iron furniture. You will love her exciting selection of authentic Mexican imports and crafts, for the home and patio. Outside, you'll find iron patio furniture with brightly-colored umbrellas, pink stone fountains, birdcages of every size and shape, and unique outdoor fireplaces. Inside, iron and glass tables are set with polished pewter and pottery, and the walls are filled with fabulous art and decorative crosses. Veldany's Gifts is open Monday-Friday 10 am-3 pm, 4-7 pm, Saturday 10 am-5 pm. Closed Tuesday. Call 956-630-3659.

Health, Beauty & Soda Fountains

Lily Majors Rambo had a desire to bring quality health food products to the people of McAllen. After visiting all of the major markets throughout the United States, and researching the finest Health Food Stores, Lily opened Major Health Foods, 1001 S. 10th Street, in 1982. It was a tiny place then—three employees and a small snack bar that served smoothies. Lily's daughter JoLynn Hasler joined her in business, and 20 years later, Major Health Foods has doubled in size and now caters to the entire Rio Grande Valley. In addition, they carry a large

assortment of body building products and vitamins with wonderful customer service. The snack bar menu has also grown. Hours are Monday-Saturday 9 am-8 pm and Sunday 10 am-6 pm. Call 956-687-7759 or visit www.majorhealthfoods.com online.

LEE'S PHARMACY

Offering the best pharmaceutical care to McAllen since 1952, Lee's Pharmacy, 1901 S. 1st, continues to grow! From the beginning, when Mr. Baldomero Vela Sr. first opened, until today with his children successfully operating two locations, Lee's Pharmacy has been dedicated to providing pharmacy services, medical equipment, and health care products to the entire Rio Grande Valley. The highly qualified staff consists of pharmacists, LVN's and respiratory therapists, utilizing the latest technology and medical information. For an extra special treat, visit the old-fashioned soda fountain. Open seven days a week from 7 am-midnight. Call 956-686-3716 or visit www.leespharmacy.com.

Hotels & Motels

 Located only one mile from the McAllen International Airport and 10 miles from the Texas-Mexico Border (Reynosa), The Hilton Garden Inn, 617 Expwy 83, is the perfect place to end a wonderful day of Valley shopping and fun. The elegant décor and friendly South Texas hospitality have earned this hotel the "Guest Loyalty Award". By focusing on what the guests want and need, they deliver the highest degree of service and cost savings to both business and leisure travelers. There are 104 guest rooms (eight suites,) a fitness center, a breakfast cafe, an outdoor pool and whirlpool, a 24-hour business center and a banquet space to accommodate 100 guests. Each room has a refrigerator, a microwave, and a coffee maker, as well as high-speed internet access and a business desk. Kids—Sony Playstation is also available! Call 956-664-2900 or 800-HILTONS; or visit www.hilton.com.

 Sometimes where a traveler chooses to spend the night may be the most important decision of the day. After a long, hard day, it is important to "come home" to spacious, comfortable rooms with amenities that say, "relax, unwind and be our guest." The Courtyard by Marriott at 2131 S. 10th Street in McAllen features 110 spacious rooms, spa rooms, and one-and-two-bedroom suites. All of the rooms have large well-lit desks, telephones with data port capabilities, in-room coffee makers, hair dryers, cable TV, and pay-per-view movies. The suites have a separate living room and small refrigerator. You'll also find a beautiful open-air courtyard with a gazebo, a cozy lounge, an exercise room, a heated swimming pool and a whirlpool. The Courtyard has received numerous service awards including the "Chairman's Award" and the "Beautification Award for Outstanding Landscaping." For reservations, call 1-888-668-7808.

The local owners and operators of The Fairfield Inn and Suites, 2117 S. 10th Street, invites you to unpack your bags, and let them do the rest to make your stay in McAllen wonderful. There are 68 bright, new spacious guest rooms with amenities to please both business and pleasure travelers. Begin the day with a very generous complimentary continental breakfast, and end the evening with room service from Tony Roma's. There is a heated pool and Jacuzzi, an exercise room, guest laundry facilities, and same-day valet service. Wonderful "freebies" include local calls, USA Today newspaper, and airport shuttle service. All rooms are equipped with two phones, Data ports and well-lit desks. It was not surprising to learn that the Fairfield Inn and Suites received the Blue Diamond Award for High Guest Satisfaction. They do it right! Call 1-866-971-9444.

Jewelry, Fashion & Accessories

DRESS BLACK

Opening Dress Black was Alandra Speights' dream come true. She has always loved the unusual. The walls in this fun, unique boutique at 5401 N. 10th Street, Suite 108, McAllen are painted bright pink and the shop is decorated in shabby chic with old wood columns. Alandra carries beautiful, comfortable clothing and sparkling accessories that will make your shopping experience a dream with lines such as BCBC Maxazaria, Hype, Ella Moss, and locally-designed-and-manufactured clothes exclusive to the store. The store is open Tuesday-Friday 11 am-7 pm, Saturday 10:30 am-5 pm. Call 956-661-8722.

RETAIL & WHOLESALE

Face it. Women love jewelry. We love it on our fingers, on our wrists, on our ears, around our necks, and even on our toes. From simple bands of silver, to strands of glittering glass beads, we love it all. Jakybon Accessories at 1424 Beaumont in McAllen, is a store filled with lovely jewelry and beaded accessories. You'll find fashion jewelry and custom designs in turquoise, coral, amber, and amethyst. Owner Juany Perez credits God for her store, and it has been a heavenly experience for her and her two daughters—for which the store is named. They are custom jewelry designers, and will work with you in choosing and designing the perfect beads and semi-precious stones. You'll also find a line of beautiful sterling silver jewelry, as well as a wonderful selection of antiques and home décor. Open Monday-Friday 10:30 am-6 pm, Saturday 'til 7 pm and Sunday 11:30 am-4 pm. Call 956-683-7226.

Look for the pretty burgundy awning at 1307 S. 10th Street in McAllen, and you've found the Rio Grande Valley's only specialty store dedicated exclusively to the plus size woman. Owner Becky Malcik travels to every market from New York to Los Angeles to Dallas in search of ever changing trends in plus size swimwear, casual, sportswear, dresses and evening gowns. She enjoys welcoming returning customers from as far north as Montreal in the winter, and as far south as Mexico City in the summer. The shop is pretty and elegant, and the soft background music creates a relaxing atmosphere for productive browsing. You'll love Becky and her staff, and you'll appreciate their attention and wonderful personal service. We know that after only one visit you'll be hooked! Her motto: Bec's Fashions … where fashion begins at size 14! Hours are Monday-Saturday 10 am-6 pm and Sunday noon-5 pm. Call 956-682-6351.

Simply By Grace

Many times the most wonderful things in life are available to us "simply by grace," so the name for this wonderful clothing boutique, 420 N. 10th Street in McAllen, is perfect in every way. Gracie Guerra specializes in high-quality new and "semi-new" ladies namebrand apparel and accessories. Gracie loves being able to help women "dress rich for only pennies." You will find it very hard to distinguish between new and semi-new here, because Gracie carries only the best brands and accepts only those items that have been kept in perfect condition. Her specialty is dressing the executive, professional woman in apparel by Jones New York, Kasper, Ellen Tracy, Carol Little, and Liz Clairborne, etc. Add the perfect handbag and shoes, and you'll be ready for anything.

You will enjoy the elegance and charm of Simply by Grace, and appreciate the friendliness and professionalism of the staff. They take time to work with each customer, dressing her to look like a million bucks on just a few dollars! Everything is so affordable, that even in today's slow economy, women can have both an extensive day and evening wardrobe. You'll also find exclusive sterling silver for the workplace, and fabulous fashion jewelry for a fun night out.

Hours are Monday-Saturday from 10 am-7 pm (late enough to shop after work.) This must-shop store is located in the Concord Shopping Center in Suite 4. Don't wait to learn how easy it is to

look fabulous for less than you would ever imagine. You'll never want to pay full price again after discovering Simply By Grace. Call 956-682-8142 for more information.

Our Secret

What started as a tiny children's consignment store in 1992 has grown into the Rio Grande Valley's star of stars—Our Secret/At Home. Obviously, owner Sandy Laurel decided not to keep the store a secret, as it has grown from 300 consigners to more than 5,500 in an 11-year span and is now a 6,300 square-foot, upscale and fast-paced store.

Our Secret offers a wide range of choices for men, women (maternity, too!) and children. All clothing items are carefully considered and critiqued before being placed in the store, then steam-pressed, and perfectly arranged by article, color and size. Our Secret also carries jewelry, accessories, shoes, handbags, as well as children's toys and infant equipment such as strollers and car seats.

As you browse through Our Secret, you'll notice an old vintage-style door that leads to At Home where you'll find treasures galore! Whether you're looking for a lovely sofa or a complete bedroom set, you'll find it here! Check  out At Home's china, crystal, fine art and deco items, too.

Sandy, Kathy, RaNae and Yesenia are selective but can't resist a fabulous find. And, they love the opportunity to offer those fabulous finds to you! If by an unusual stroke of bad luck you don't see what you're looking for, be sure to come back, as the selection  changes daily. Our Secret/At Home is located at 5207 N. McColl Road, in McAllen. Hours are Monday-Friday 10 am-6 pm and Saturday 10 am-5 pm. Call 956-686-5437.

Joyce's International Boutique

Do you love to shop for elite designer clothes? Then, you'll love Joyce's International Boutique. This trendy store is a hot spot for specialty buys and great prices on select designer fashions.

Located in the bustling downtown area, 120 S. Broadway in McAllen, Joyce's International Boutique's owner works especially hard to find the best prices on even the most exclusive designer clothes, all to make sure that her customers get the very best deals.

Housed in this beautifully-restored 1950's building is a goldmine of deals, sales and specialty items that are one-of-a-kind finds. You'll discover a great selection of Fendi, Versace, Christian Dior and Gucci. From deisigner lines of clothing, handbags and accessories to designer fragrances for both men and women, you'll need an extra suitcase to hold all your purchases.

Joyce's International Boutique also offers a great collection of cosmetics. After being in the business for 15 years, the staff has definitely learned about quality customer service. Each friendly salesperson is there to make your day of shopping even more enjoyable. And, to help ensure this, Joyce's International Boutique offers after hours shopping for their out-of-town guests. Simply call and tell a representative from the boutique when it would be best for you to stop by, and the staff-members will do their best to make that available to you.

Joyce's International Boutique is open Monday-Saturday 10 am-7 pm and Sunday 11 am-6 pm. For more information, call 956-971-0611.

Restaurants, Gourment & Specialty Foods

Chilé Piquin Cafe, 125 Nolana in McAllen, is known for more than simply its great food. The eclectic South Texas décor offers a great atmosphere honoring the rich heritage of the Rio Grande Valley. The walls are lined with posters celebrating Texas *conjunto* festivals, as well as antique labels taken from the crates used by the growers of the Rio Grande Valley to distinguish their fruit and vegetables in the market place. Owner, Gloria Alvarado has chosen to keep the tradition alive in the restaurant's own logo, showing her commitment not only to honor her heritage, but also to use fresh Valley products. Experience what the people of McAllen have voted as their Favorite Mexican Food, their Favorite Fajitas, and the Friendliest Restaurant in town. Whether it's the well-known Puffy Tacos or one of their specialties—The Pachanga Chicken—you'll enjoy great food in a great atmosphere. Hours are Monday-Saturday 7 am-10 pm, and Sunday 9 am-4 pm. Make sure you check out the other location in Pharr at the El Centro Mall. Call 956-631-3838 in McAllen or 956-787-2424 in Pharr.

For 20 years, City Café & Catering has been the Rio Grande Valley's choice for Fresh Homemade Soups, Salads, Pastas, Pizzas, and Sandwiches. That's quite an order to fill, and Cynthia McRae does it deliciously! In fact, she has been serving wonderful, quality food for 20 years. Choose from delicious quiche, quesadillas, Texas style chicken salad, and the spicy Southwest pasta for lunch. You can order to go, too! City Café & Catering is located at 2901 N. 10th Street in McAllen, and is now serving really trendy and unusual dinner entrees along with beer and wine. Hours are Monday-Saturday 10 am-8:30 pm and Sunday 11 am-3 pm. Call 956-682-8737.

SAHADI

LE BISTRO · FINE WINES · GOURMET FOODS

Rated one of the top five restaurants in McAllen, Sahadi Café's reputation for exciting and unique Mediterranean cuisine and beverages extends throughout the Rio Grande Valley. Mr. and Mrs. John Sahadi opened the specialty food store in 1973, and added the restaurant in 1989, at its current location, 709 N. 10th Street. You will not find another place like this in this region—a gourmet store and a café in the same place. You'll find more than 700 wine labels hand-picked by the owner, which can be included in the wonderful Sahadi gourmet gift baskets.

The Sahadi Café offers a delightful variety of foods from the Mediterranean region: escargot (Burgundy snails), Greek Gyros, Italian hoagies, Middle East Feast, and scratch-made soups based on family recipes. The salads are made with the freshest ingredients including baby leaf lettuces, cheeses, olives, tomatoes, and homemade dressings. Sahadi's also creates beautiful and delicious party trays. For those with a sweet tooth, the bakery produces a variety of Middle Eastern pastries, as well as 20 different cakes, including the Sahadi signature "Tres Leches" cake and various cheesecakes. Jeffrey Sahadi, with the honor and respect for his father who started this institution so many years ago, is pleased to run the business.

The store is open Monday-Thursday 10 am-7 pm, until 9:30 pm on Friday, until 7:30 pm on Saturday, and on Sunday noon-6 pm. The restaurant is open Monday 11 am-6 pm; Tuesday-Thursday 11 am-10 pm; Friday 11 am-midnight; Saturday 11 am-11 pm and Sunday noon-6 pm. Call 956-682-3419.

The Blue Onion house pizza sauce is a combination of slow roasted tomatoes, onions, and garlic with a slightly smoky flavor, seasoned with oregano, basil, and chipolté peppers. Add that to their grilled pizza dough or flatbreads, sprinkle on a few toppings, and you'll understand why the restaurant has such a large following. Everything is delicious! The Blue Onion, at 925 Dove Avenue in McAllen and 2017 W. Expwy 83 in Weslaco, was the result of a long-time dream of owner Eric Arndt. This former Science teacher just knew that this would be something the Valley would love—he was right. The chefs have gathered the freshest ingredients and most interesting influences from around the world to create new and exciting dishes. Open Monday-Thursday and Sunday 11 am-9 pm and Friday-Saturday until 10 pm. Call 956-682-9884 in McAllen or 956-447-0067 in Weslaco.

The best way to describe Sweet Temptations at 5401 N. 10th Street in McAllen is to tell you a few of the incredible things on the menu. Breakfast includes heavenly pancakes, breakfast quiche, cinnamon rolls, and omelets, and of course, gourmet coffees. For lunch, try cream soups, fresh salads, sandwiches on homemade breads, lasagna, Parmesan chicken or meatloaf. But save room for delicious desserts like apple dumpling or New York cheesecake. Owners Harry and Esmeralda Urey have just opened the building's second floor as an intimate dining room, and it is the perfect place for a romantic dinner. Soft lighting, original artwork, candles, centerpieces, and beautiful music create a wonderful atmosphere. Cocktails are all "top shelf," and the cuisine is excellent. Just plan to take your time and enjoy the complete experience. Hours are Monday-Saturday 7 am-9 pm. Call 956-630-0307.

BOB STARK'S BEEF SHOP

Get out the gourmet and wild game cookbooks, or just light up the backyard grill. You'll find the largest assortment, and the most delicious cuts of meat you could ever imagine at Bob Stark's Beef Shop, 707 Dove Street in McAllen. Customers drive from throughout the Valley for the shop's famous award-winning Sirloin Marinated Fajitas; Beef, Chicken and Shrimp Kabobs; and the thick cuts of Iowa Beef. The long meat counter is filled with favorites, as well as hard-to-find meat and fowl such as: buffalo, quail, veal, lamb, rabbit, duck, geese, pheasant, venison, fish, shrimp and frog legs. That should keep even the most imaginative backyard chef busy throughout the year.

The store is open Monday-Saturday 9 am-7 pm and Sunday 10 am-4 pm. Bob Stark's guarantees the finest cuts of meat and friendly customized service at supermarket prices. For more information, call 956-682-9331.

MARBLE SLAB CREAMERY

Owner Maya Advani credits her niece, Mrs. Kavita Arvind Melwani, for her adventure into the ice cream business! After tasting the delicious Marble Slab homemade ice cream, she convinced Maya to open a shop in McAllen. If you have never been inside a Marble Slab Creamery, or tasted its ice cream, frozen yogurt and fresh-baked goods, run don't walk, to 4100 N. 2nd Street for an extraordinary experience!

Create your own ice cream fantasy by first choosing your favorite ice cream, then selecting your "mixins" and watching as they are folded together on the signature marble slab and finally piled atop of a chocolate dipped waffle cone. Or treat yourself to delicious made-from-scratch cookies, pies, and brownies. Oh yes, don't forget to try one of Marble Slab's gourmet coffees! The creamery is open Monday-Thursday, and Sunday from 11 am-10:30 pm, Friday-Saturday until 11 pm. Call 956-631-7915.

THE BLUE SHELL

Be sure and check out The Blue Shell in McAllen, at these locations 3817 N. 10th Street and 4009 N. 23rd Street. See page 21 for full details.

Salons, Spas & Indulgence

The goal of the entire staff at Face Body Bath & Beyond at 2901 N. 10th Street in McAllen, is to revitalize you—"face, body, and beyond!" The spa, medically directed by Dr. Donald Hall, offers products and procedures that are on the cutting edge in the beauty industry. Microdermabrasion, cellulite reduction, and permanent cosmetics, are available as well as botox and collagen injections. Massage therapy, facials, chemical peels, body wraps, manicures and pedicures are also available. Whether you need help with skin problems, weight loss, or a total rejuvenation of your body, owner Barbara Hall can help you "start today" in finding the beautiful person you are inside. Hours are Monday-Friday 9 am-7 pm and Saturday until 6 pm. Call 956-994-9881.

LASER CLINIC

Located only a few blocks from the border crossing, directly behind the Hotel Grand Premiere is a beautiful, elegant facility known throughout Mexico as one of the top cosmetic clinics in the country. Dr. Raúl López and his professional staff invite you to visit their beautiful offices in Reynosa and learn about the many cosmetic surgical services they provide.

The lobby and rooms are beautifully furnished and decorated with elegance and comfort in mind. Even the surgery and recovery rooms are personalized with fine furniture, pretty linens and fresh flowers. You'll feel extremely pampered by the caring staff while you receive the expert care of Dr. Raúl López.

Dr. López is a Member de la Asociación Mexicana de Cirugia Plastica Estética y Reconstructiva, A.C. and is "Certificado por el Consejo Mexicano de Cirugia Plástica." He is recognized throughout Mexico as one of the top doctors in this field. His expertise includes: liposuction; facial cosmetics; breast augmentation, reduction, and reconstruction; Botox treatments; and microdermabrasion.

Visit the web-site at www.laserclinic.com.mx to learn more about each procedure and have a visual tour of the facility. For more information or reservations, please telephone the U.S. number, 956-810-7914. You will be treated with the utmost respect and confidentiality. And, you'll be extremely pleased with the professional, yet personal attention to your wants and needs. Go ahead and call—a new you awaits!

Specialty Shops, Sports & Fitness

Next time you're putting together a family album or a special presentation for work, keep Copy It! in mind. It is a full service copy place, offering binding, photocopies, and personalized invitations.

From supplies to ideas, Copy It! helps take your creative dreams to paper realities. The store window is cleverly displayed with new ideas and designs for your scrapbook, and the helpful staff will show you what you need to make each idea your own.

Conveniently placed in the Tiffany shopping center, Copy It!, 1001 S. 10th Street Suite F in McAllen, is the only copy facility on the southside of town.

Copy It! is open Monday-Friday 7 am-10 pm, Saturday 9 am-10 pm and Sunday noon-10 pm. For more information, call 956-664-0599.

Cimarron

The Club at Cimarron
Be sure and check out this great fitness center in Mission, at 1200 S. Shary Road. See page 98 for full details.

DISCOVER MISSION

Bienvenidos! You will hear this greeting from almost everyone in Mission, Texas as the friendly townspeople invite you to "Savor the culture, climate, color and charm of Mission!" Located in the lower Rio Grande Valley at the southern tip of Texas, Mission is easily accessible from all parts of Texas, the United States, Canada, and Mexico. It is a unique city, with all the charm of small-town southern hospitality, yet with the amenities of a large city. The cultures blend easily, as the people share common interests and goals, yet retain their unique identities and personalities. Recreational and educational opportunities abound in this colorful, comfortable town.

SAVOR THE HISTORY

When the Spanish government began to settle the area from the Panuco River in Tampico, Mexico to the Nueces River in present-day Corpus Christi, the site known as La Lomita was granted to Captain Cantu of Reynosa. In 1865, La Lomita Mission was built on the river south of the settlement, which later became the city of Mission.

In recent history, you'll probably recognize this famous "Mission Legend" who grew up to be the coach of the Dallas Cowboys for 30 years—Coach Tom Landry. Landry was born in 1924 in the town of Mission and played quarterback for the Mission Eagles. A football scholarship took him to the University of Texas in 1942, but the war interrupted his college career. After serving in the Army Air Corps as a pilot, he returned to Texas, and of course, football. The rest … as they say, is history. He served as a coach for the New York Giants for a few years and then headed for Dallas in 1969. It was during his 30 years with the Cowboys that they became known as "America's Team." In 1993, Mission residents Bill and Gen Long commissioned artist Manuel Hinojosa, to create the Tom Landry Mural, which measures 95 x 18 feet, and adorns the north exterior of a building that faces Tom Landry Boulevard. It was commissioned by Coach Landry himself who said, "The mural depicts my life from my birth in Mission to the Pro Football Hall of Fame. It's really nice to have something like this from your hometown." Ladies, I promise that your guys will not mind tagging along for this one!

SAVOR THE SIGHTS AND EVENTS!

Carve out a nice bit of time to see and do all of the wonderful things in Mission. The La Lomita Chapel, a historic site on the National Registry, is located at a city park near the Rio Grande. And, Bensten State Park offers most of the Valley "specialties" with 587 acres of lush and densely wooded river-bottom lands, reminiscent of South Texas' wildlife refuges. Camping facilities, picnic areas, and full hookups are available. The park was named after another famous native son, Senator Lloyd Bensten. Because birdwatchers have been able to record more than 400 bird species in the area, this state park is the site of the World Birding Center, which includes interactive educational displays, trails with feeding stations, and viewing towers. Beginner birders to experts will enjoy the special lectures, guided tours and educational opportunities offered at this beautiful center. From colorful hummingbird gardens to remote wilderness areas, the Center offers a diverse birding experience.

Mission is also known to have recorded more than 300 butterfly species in the area, garnering the privilege of being named the future site for a 100-acre Butterfly Park by the North America Butterfly Association. This world-class outdoor natural habitat will be designed to attract and establish populations of rare south Texas species. A Texas Butterfly Festival is held each October in Mission, where guests hear from internationally-renowned speakers, see butterflies in their natural habitats on expert-guided field trips, and are able to stock up on butterfly and nature merchandise. Kids will enjoy the Butterfly Costume Parade, and Butterfly Bonanza.

One of the most-loved and best-attended festivals in Mission is the Texas Citrus Fiesta, which attracts thousands of spectators from around the nation. For more than 60 years, revelers have enjoyed three days of festivities including the famous "Parade of Oranges" with floats and bands; a carnival; Texas BBQ; live music; food booths; art and craft displays; and an educational fun fair.

For more information on Mission, call the Greater Mission Chamber of Commerce at 800-580-2700 or 956-585-2727 or visit www.missionchamber.com.

Mission Fairs Festivals & Fun

January
Texas Citrus Fiesta

February
Winter Texan Fiesta

April
Annual Spring Gala

October
Texas Butterfly Festival

Antiques

MARIA LOUISA'S ANTIQUES, BOOKS & COLLECTIBLES

As a retired educator, Maria Louisa Garcia's long time dream had been to open a used bookstore. From her collection of rare books, Maria Louisa's at 2708-A E. Griffin Pkwy in Mission has evolved into a charming, collector's paradise. Items range from a turn-of-the-century piano, antique bottles and art to "not so old" but "good as gold" consignment items. Hours are Monday-Friday 8 am-6 pm, Saturday 9 am-6 pm and Sunday 1-5 pm. Call 956-664-9350 or visit www.daamars.com.

HIDDEN TREASURES

As her business grew over 20 years, Minnie Saenz kept moving her "Hidden Treasures" to bigger buildings. She started with a little 5 x 5 corner across from the Post Office, and now has 8,000 square feet with more than 10 indoor stores and 12 booths at 215 W. 9th Street in Mission. You can't miss the brightly-painted building with antiques lining the sidewalk. You'll find a variety of antiques from furniture to toys. Hours are Monday-Saturday 10 am-6 pm. Call 956-580-6700.

Art, Artists, Fashion & Specialty Shops

Glassica Alan Leidner is carrying on the legacy of creating beautiful stained glass art—just as he learned from the master craftsman who taught him the art-form years ago. Life-long to the valley, Leidner has a talent for interpreting the beauty of this unique part of the country, and shaping it into the colorful pieces of glass art displayed throughout the gallery. His creations include stained glass, as well as beveled glass and etched glass panels for entryways, kitchens, dining rooms, bathrooms, bar areas and cabinetry. He prides himself on being able to create original art-work based on the customer's individual tastes, style and budget, saying, " … it doesn't cost any more to get a piece of custom made art—exactly how a person wants it."

Glassica, is located at 2011 School Lane in Mission, and is open Monday-Friday 8 am-5 pm. For more information, call 956-581-8774 or visit www.glassica.com online.

Scented Rocks by Ginger

When Ginger Silva started her potpourri business, she had to lug really heavy rocks from door to door. The hard work was well worth the effort, because her success has been very sweet! People began buying her "scented rocks" and oils so fast that she soon opened a shop, Scented Rocks by Ginger, at 1400 E. 22nd Street in Mission, along with her store the Bargain Bazaar in McAllen at 4400 N. 23rd. Scented Rocks was even featured in the March 2003 issue of *Today's Latina*, which is quite an honor.

In addition to the rocks, Ginger carries a collection of potpourri, many wonderful unique gift items; and more than 40 fragrance oils. The best method for scenting a larger area is an electric aroma lamp—which has a ceramic top with a small dip for fragrance oils—made exclusively for Scented Rocks. The store is open daily, 10 am-6 pm and weekends at Bargain Bazaar. Call 956-581-6973 or visit www.scentedrocks.com.

BIRD HOUSES BY PHYLLIS

Peep into the driveway and yard of Phyllis Weatherford, and you'll see birdhouses made from every imaginable material. After making birdhouses for friends and family for several years, she began to get so many requests that her business went "to the  birds!" She uses items most people consider to be trash—old door-knobs, doorjambs, license plates, pieces of rusted hardware, and wood she finds in the most unusual places to make birdhouses of every shape and size. A sign on her door at 404 E. Griffin Pkwy in Mission tells customers to "Honk for Help," and if you don't find what you are looking for there, she will custom design a birdhouse especially for you. Chances are though; you'll find something you love. Select from the Cowboy Boot House, the Church House, the Texas Flag House, or Flower Power House to name a few. Phyllis takes "junk" and turns it into gems. Call 956-580-4669.

Utilizing her degree in Fiber Arts from the University of Oregon, Nancy Algrim's artistic touch is evident in every carefully selected piece of clothing and jewelry at the Black Iris, 1400 N. Bryan Road in Mission.

The contemporary natural fiber apparel and wearable art collection is great fun because the pieces are as unique as the individuals who choose them. Nancy's objective is to provide you with a personalized shopping experience attending to your needs as only a fine boutique can.

Beautiful pieces of Art Glass jewelry are created on-site in the studio. Nancy and her husband Curtis Whatley use a 4000° torch to form beads from Italian Murrano Glass. These beads are then used to make jewelry that will endure for generations.

Hours are Monday-Saturday 10 am-5:30 pm, and Friday 11 am-6 pm. For more information, call 956-519-3190.

Bed & Breakfasts & Resorts

EL ROCIO RETREAT CENTER

As the wrought iron gate swings open, you'll find your senses awaken to a magical atmosphere of peace and tranquility, and be captivated by the timeless beauty that is—El Rocio. This unique Mission resort and retreat center is located at 2519 S. Inspiration Road on 18 acres of incredibly beautiful flora and fauna—truly a wildlife photographer's dream. In fact, El Rocio is winner of the 2002 Valley Land Fund Photography Contest. The World Birding Center is just three miles away, and golfers may take advantage of the 18-hole golf course at the adjacent Seven Oaks Country Club. Inside the main house, which was hand crafted around a huge "tree of life," beautiful mosaic tiles, chandeliers, statuary, fountains, and antique religious articles create an intimate ambiance. Guests may enjoy cowboy chuckwagon dinners and even take a horse-drawn carriage ride around the property. Visit www.elrocioretreat.com or call 956-584-7432.

Entertainment, Golf, Sports, & Fitness

The Club at Cimarron

The easy elegant atmosphere of The Club at Cimarron is absolutely perfect for special dinners, social and business meetings or seminars, or private parties for 10 to 500 guests. The formal dining area overlooks the beautiful golf course, and the fireside lounge is intimate and warm. Fitness memberships are also available, which include access to four racquetball courts, eight tennis courts, and an Olympic size pool. The golf course is a Championship 18-hole course designed by Dave Bennett, and the Pro Shop is fully stocked with name-brand merchandise. Summertime offers camps for children with sports activities, crafts, and lots of fun. And, there are continuous league tournaments throughout the year, as well as personal classes in eight tennis, racquetball, aerobics, karate, and art. The Club at Cimarron is located at 1200 S. Shary Road in Mission. Call 956-581-7401 or visit www.clubatcimarron.com.

Ask anyone throughout the state of Texas about the South Texas Stallions, and chances are they'll know you are talking about one of the top, championship sports organizations in the state. Rick and Ileana Martinez, owners of the Sports Locker Athletic Store at 2002 N. Conway in Mission, are actively involved in the Texas Stallions organization. This includes coaching boys and girls basketball, baseball, and cheerleading toward national competition. They carry sports equipment and uniforms for any sport, and furnish personalization for teams and individuals. Sports Locker is known throughout the Valley for its "Kind of Embroidery," for caps, T's, jackets, or bags. You'll find everything you need from socks and shoes to water bottles and headgear. It is a one-stop shop for all of your athletic equipment needs. Open Monday-Friday 10 am-7 pm, and Saturday 10 am-3 pm. Call 956-580-4488.

THE BORDER THEATRE

It's the "stuff" movies are made of … and if they did make a movie about the lives of Jeannie and Robert Pena and their fairytale romance, they could show it right here at The Border Theatre, 905 Conway. It is a story about a young boy meeting a young girl in an old movie theatre where they both worked; falling in love there; and in the end, having the opportunity to buy the histori- cal theatre where they first kissed and pledged their love to each other.

The historical Border Theatre not only served as the perfect back drop for many romances, but also has provided three genera- tions of residents and visitors with the finest in family entertainment in one of the last theatres of its kind in Texas. It opened April 3, 1942, with the Gene Autry movie, "Heart of the Rio Grande." How appropriate! It is virtually the same inside and out as it was when constructed, except for the Cinemascope screen added in 1967. It has a seating capacity of 393 and a snack bar in the main lobby where moviegoers can treat themselves to hot dogs, popcorn, candy, and drinks. The Border Theatre has retained the reputation as a "family movie theater," where parents can take their children, confi- dent of the kind of movie they will see. The folks of Mission say that their town would not be the same without The Border, and the Penas believe with all of their hearts that they would not be together if not for those romantic hand-holding rendezvous in the theatre. Since they bought it, they have begun to see an increased interest in the old theatre, with the townspeople forming long lines to see movies like "E.T." and "Spiderman." Robert and Jeannie are happy that The Border Theatre is "claiming a new generation of fans!" It is open Monday-Friday 7 am-11 p.m., Saturday-Sunday 2-11 p.m. For more information or to arrange a tour, call 956-585-4122.

Florists, Gifts & Home Décor

ZOILA'S CREATIONS

Whether you are planning a small backyard birthday party for "los niños," or a huge party for hundreds of special friends, you absolutely must visit this floral and gift shop at 116 W. Tom Landry Street in Mission. Zoila's Creations is the place to go for beautiful decorations and superb customer service.

Zoila and Angel Garza put their hearts into everything they do, and this attention to detail has made them quite popular in Mission. They have romantic decorations for weddings, unique items for traditional quinceñeras, and fabulous balloon arches that make any party festive. You can peruse pictures of their creative work for ideas, or bring something you want them to copy. Be sure to ask about their custom-made piñatas! You'll love meeting the Garzas. They are friendly, helpful, and very creative. The store is open Tuesday-Saturday 10 am-7 pm. For information, call 956-424-1430.

Truly a "shopping event!" This wonderful home decor and specialty gift boutique at 2600 E. Griffin Pkwy in Mission has a little of everything you might want for your home, displayed brilliantly in beautifully decorated rooms. Renee's of Sharyland should be your first stop for home and office decorating and unique gifts for every occasion. Renee Martin shops New York City, Dallas, Los Angeles and San Francisco to bring you a very interesting collection of items at very reasonable prices.

You'll find the most wonderful body and bath products by Thyme's and a large selection of Colonial Candles for every room in your home. She carries Possible Dreams Collectibles, Arthur Court pewter, New Cannon Farms Texas Gourmet, and crosses from around the world. Unusual mirrors, frames, lamps, and woodcarvings make great gifts, and the furniture is spectacular. Renee's is also famous for its wonderful, unique gift baskets customized to your instructions, featuring Texas Gourmet Foods and Texas Wines—something perfect for everyone on your gift list. From unique children's toys and hand-made pottery to precious stone and sterling jewelry and fashion accessories, you'll love the unusual selections that make shopping Renee's of Sharyland such a treat.

Café Renee, a gourmet coffeehouse, restaurant and bakery, is now open for breakfast and lunch. Enjoy homemade pastries including Texas-size caramel rolls, wonderful homemade soups served in breadbowls and incredible desserts such as grapefruit pie—a local favorite. Hours are Monday-Saturday 8 am-6 pm with extended holiday hours. Call 956-519-9595 or visit www.reneemartin.com.

(Featured on back cover.)

The Gift Garden

From glorious bouquets of fragrant roses, to arrangements of exotic flowers, to seasonal creations that will brighten your holidays—The Gift Garden should be your first stop. This beautiful gift, home décor and floral shop is located at 2421 E. Griffin Pkwy, and has been a favorite Mission florist for 14 years. You'll find a beautiful selection of home and garden items like crosses and angels; a large selection of baby and children's gifts; Texas souvenirs; jewelry; Hallmark cards; stationary; gift-wrap and exciting holiday decorations. Owners J.B. and Debbie Townsend are dedicated to personal service and assisting you with a special need or occasion. Hours are Monday-Saturday 9 am-6 pm. For more information, visit www.giftgardenflorist.com or call 956-581-7541 or 800-676-1030.

BROADWAY HARDWARE & GIFTS

One of the things you will love most about Broadway Hardware, 114 W. 9th Street in Mission is the store's new comprehensive selection of cutlery, including: kitchen, sporting, and agricultural knives. The newly renovated housewares and gifts departments offer, the typical "hardware"—nuts, bolts, and tools, as well as unique gift items. Great merchandise, and the best customer service in town! Call 956-585-4831. *(Color picture featured in front section of the book.)*

Furniture

Cash & Carry Home Furnishings

Ed and Mary Gomez were in the home building business in Austin for many years before making Mission their home. They opened their furniture store at 1005 N. Conway in 1990, with a desire to provide quality furniture at affordable prices, as well as offer great customer service. They sure did something right! The Mission folks voted Cash & Carry Home Furnishings their No. 1 furniture store! Stop by, and you'll understand why.

The Gomez family recognizes and appreciates the continued support from their friends and customers—especially the Winter Texans who have become repeat visitors over the years. People keep coming back because they know they will find beautiful furniture and accessories at reasonable prices. And, they enjoy the personal attention they are given each time they walk through the doors of Cash & Carry Home Furnishings. The Gomez's invite the "Lady's Day Out" readers to come and spend time in their beautiful store, and see the wonderful rooms of furniture and home accessories. The staff is very friendly and competent, and truly interested in helping people find the right pieces for their home, office or ranch.

Whether you are looking for bedroom, dining room, or living room furniture, you will love the large selection of complete sets or individual pieces. They will be incorporating more antique pieces into their line this year, giving Cash & Carry Home Furnishings a more "Victorian Style," featuring great classic furniture. Stop by Monday-Saturday 9 am-6 pm., or call 956-584-7256 for more information.

RUSTIC FURNITURE EXCLUSIVE

The spirit of Mexico and the Old West lives on in the unique hand-carved furniture you'll find at Rustic Furniture Exclusive, 4109 N. Conway A-9. Owners Carlos and Iliana Vela have three furniture stores in Mexico where the furniture and home accessories are built.

Now with their beautiful showroom in Mission, they can offer their customers—wholesale and retail alike—the same unique and wonderfully hand-made pieces that they feature in their stores South of the border. The large warehouse is filled with pieces made from Mesquite wood, old doors from turn-of-the-century buildings, and wrought iron.

Whether you are looking for headboards, armoires, dining room tables and curios, or entertainment centers, you will love the large, unusual selection of rustic furniture. This rustic look blends so well with the lifestyles of the Rio Grande Valley families. Maybe that's why the Velas have so many return customers.

The Velas understand and cater to their connection to the land. Rustic Furniture Exclusive reflects a perfect blend of Mexico and

Texas. The result? Absolute irresistible rustic furnishings. Customers also enjoy the opportunity to custom design their own pieces. Rustic Furniture Exclusive is open seven days a week from 10 am-7 pm. For more information, call 956-583-4833.

A.V. FURNITURE

This is a true "Mom and Pop" shop. Albino and Claudia Villarreal have owned A.V. Furniture in Mission for more than ten years, and have gained a reputation as honest and sincere owners who really care about their customers' needs. The Villarreals had always loved shopping flea markets and finding unique antiques and unusual furniture, so it was only natural for the twosome to open their own furniture store, where they could sell both old and new pieces. A.V. Furniture Store is located 2- miles West of Expwy 83 in a 15,000 square foot building. The Villarreals keep up with the latest trends in fine furniture, and carry lines that are traditional and classic, such as Ashley and Hart. Customers love that every-

thing in the store is so reasonably priced, and show their appreciation by returning again and again. Hours are Monday-Saturday 10 am-7 pm. Call 956-581-5432 to learn more.

Hotels

EXECUTIVE INN & SUITES

Located in the lush semi-tropical lower Rio Grande Valley, the Executive Inn & Suites at 1786 W. Hwy 83 in Mission is only a short distance from the bright sandy beaches of South Padre Island, Falcon Lake or Old Mexico. The Inn offers 50 spacious ground-floor rooms with cable, HBO and 24-hour phone service. And, the king suites have a mini fridge and 27-inch screen television. There is also an on-site restaurant, guest laundry services and a swimming pool; and pets are welcome for a small additional fee. The owners are always on the premises. Their mission? To make each guest feel like family. For reservations or more information, call 956-581-7451. Bienvenidos Amigos!

Restaurants & Tearooms

VICTORIA'S ANTIQUES & TEA ROOM

When Victoria Lopez first opened her shop, she knew exactly what she wanted—elegance, a welcoming relaxing atmosphere, and a ladylike experience. Victoria's Antiques and Tearoom meets that criteria and more.

The tranquil background music makes great company while browsing through the beautifully displayed antiques and gifts. After taking your time walking through the various treasures, you can relax with a cup of tea and a sweet treat. Located at 1524 N. Conway in Mission, it's open Tuesday-Saturday 10 am-5 pm. To find out more about this great hide away, call 956-583-8686.

El PATIO Restaurant

When the entire family is involved in running a restaurant, the result is usually a very popular and successful business. This is certainly true of El Patio Restaurant at 2003 N. Conway in Mission. Mario Garza and his whole famlia are involved in running the restaurant, making sure that the chips are always hot and plentiful and the coffee is always hot. Mario says that education has played a large part in the success of the business. He trains the staff in food preparation and service, and as a result the customers keep coming back!

El Patio is best known for its Botana Platters, Mexican Plates, homemade caldos, and the popular buffets, but what we remember best is that the entire experience was so much fun. The food was delicious, the atmosphere bright and joyful, and the wait staff extremely friendly.

We were surprised to learn that Mario Garza was relatively new to the restaurant business. With everything so perfect and professional at El Patio, you'd think Mario had grown up in the restaurant business. Actually, Mario was a banker for 35 years before taking the plunge into the food business. Obviously his hard work, organizational capabilities, and determination have enabled him to learn the restaurant business very quickly. His desire now is to continue to improve the décor of the restaurant, and the whole family is helping.

El Patio is a very family-oriented restaurant, as evidenced by the throngs of families there. The Mexican Buffets are family favorites—and are available every day except Saturday. Regular hours for the restaurant are Sunday-Saturday 6 am-10 pm. From Huevos Rancheros and breakfast tacos in the morning to the sizzling fajitas, arroz y frijoles for dinner, you will love every dish. Mario and the entire Garza family invite you and your family to join them for a delicious meal and an unforgettable evening. Call 956-519-8575.

People "in the know" have their eyes on this very popular and successful steakhouse in Mission. La Tejana Steakhouse, 1215 E. Expwy 83, is growing in popularity as fast as the chef can grill their fresh, thick, perfectly-cut steaks.

Unlike most steakhouse restaurants where steaks are served with steak sauce and rolls, La Tejana remains true to the way Latinos enjoy steaks—topped with spicy salsa, and served with beans *a la charra* and home-made tortillas. The meat derives from their very own meat market in Palmview, so the cuts are of the highest quality. Diners choose their rib eyes, filet mignons, or other traditional cuts from a glass-cased refrigerated display, and the cooks stand at an open grill preparing each one right before their eyes. Although the steaks are the "main event," you will also love the house specialties like Baby Back Ribs, Quail, Lamb, Fajitas, and Mollejas. Barbecue and burgers round out the main menu, but be sure to save room for a piece of Gourmet Turtle Cheesecake or Bourbon Pecan Pie or, take a piece home for later.

The ambiance at La Tejana is truly a cultural experience. Festive "cantores" play their favorite corridos and rancheras, evoking the spirit of Old Mexico. The stone walls and pillars, beautifully carved woodwork, and dark hardwood floors, provide a warm, comfortable atmosphere, and the staff is friendly and very attentive. La Tejana has been given four stars by critics who are sure they will see this fabulous restaurant sweep the nation with its exceptional *comida*. Hours are Sunday-Thursday 11 am-11 pm and Friday-Saturday 11 am-1 am. A banquet facility and meeting room is available. To learn more, call 956-581-9312.

Salons, Spas & Cosmetics

MERLE NORMAN COSMETICS

For more than 50 years, Rio Grande Valley ladies have enjoyed the benefits of Merle Norman Cosmetics. It's no wonder the studio received the Mayoral Proclamation and is recognized as a Gold Medallion Studio for its high level of excellence and outstanding customer service. Merle Norman experts are always on hand to teach and demonstrate how to achieve the most beautiful results from their wonderful products.

Studio owner Dendea L. Balli comes from a long line of dedicated Merle Norman users. Her grandmother has used Merle Norman products for more than 60 years! Dendea grew up sampling the "gifts with purchase" from Merle Norman and was introduced to skin care as an adolescent. They are walking advertisements!

Experience a world of Beauty with Merle Norman Cosmetics, 110 E. Griffin Parkway in Mission. Hours of operation are Monday-Saturday 10 am-6 pm. To learn the latest makeup techniques, sample the latest colors or schedule an appointment, call 956-583-3700 or visit www.merlenorman.com.

MASSAGE & SPA

"One Stop, One Shop, Find It All & Have a Ball!" Mother and daughter owners Janie and Jody Buentello invite you to visit Massage and Spa at 2013 N. Conway in Mission where you will find five businesses ready to make you look and feel wonderful. Together, Janie and Jody have 11 years experience in Swedish massage, Reflexology, and Aromatherapy. You'll also find Irma's Hair Solution, O.P.I. Nails, Bella Kara Skin Care, and Herbs, Teas & Magic. Gift certificates are also available. Open Monday-Saturday 9 am-7 pm. Call 956-584-0080.

DISCOVER
SOUTH PADRE ISLAND/PORT ISABEL
Los Fresnos

Imagine a beautiful tropical island with miles of sparkling beaches, warm water, and very friendly natives. Imagine sailing, fishing, windsurfing, dolphin watching, and horseback riding from sunrise to sunset. And imagine, when the sun does settle over the ocean, evenings filled with dining, dancing and music. Welcome to paradise—welcome to South Padre Island!

The Island is 34 miles of sugar white sand bordered to the east by the Gulf of Mexico and to the west by the Laguna Madre bay, and considered throughout the United States to be one of America's top 10 beaches. It is "Where Texans kick their boots off," where visitors from all walks of life find solace in the sun, and where dreams come true for all who love to play in the water or soar through the sky. The many conveniences and attractions of this Texas resort, coupled with the incredible beauty of its pristine island terrain, draw thousands of visitors each year—some who decide never to leave. Bob St. John, author of "South Padre: The Island and Its People" states, "(South Padre Island) is a place which seems to become what you want it to be and something that you can take with you no matter where you go, and that you can talk about and relive the time you had there and think about the ones that are to come."

Makes you want to hop in your car and head there, doesn't it? Well…why don't you? Paradise awaits…

A RICH HISTORY

The actual recorded history of South Padre Island dates back as far as 1519, when Alonso Alvarez de Pineda sailed past the Isla

Blanca (White Island) while charting the Gulf of Mexico for the King of Spain. Early stories claimed that "giants" inhabited the island, which were later discovered to be the Karankawa Indians or Kronks, as they were nicknamed. They were a very tall and fierce tribe of Indians who were suspected to be cannibals. Relax, they are extinct!

When Herman Cortez conquered the Aztecs during the 1520s, gold and silver were being mined in Mexico and shipped to Spain. But, many galleons loaded with treasure were blown off course to the Island, where they foundered on sandbars. The knowledge of this great wealth afloat near the Island enticed pirates and buccaneers who preyed on Spanish ships. One of the most famous pirates, of course, was Jean Lafitte, who became a hero of the War of 1812. Legend says that he filled his casks with fresh water from a well dug just west of Laguna Madre. This historic well lies in the quiet village of Laguna Vista, just a few miles from Port Isabel.

An actual settlement was not recorded until 1804, when Padre Jose Nicolas Balli, a Catholic Missionary priest, founded Rancho Santa Cruz on the Island where he raised cattle and horses. This later became know as Padre Island. In more recent history, the Port Mansfield Gulf Channel was completed in 1964, separating South Padre Island from Padre Island. And, in 1974 the completed 2.5-mile Queen Isabella Causeway connected South Padre Island with the mainland. This is the longest bridge in Texas, and it has paved the way for the development you will see today on South Padre Island. Be careful, because many who cross the Causeway as tourists, never go back! It is said, "Once you drink the water from the Rio Grande, you will always come back, whether for a visit, or a lifetime!"

FUN IN THE SUN!

The year-round moderate temperatures make South Padre Island the ideal spot for vacationers who love to play in the sun. Whether you are looking for a weekend get-a-way, a great place to spend a college spring break, or a warm spot to winter during the cold months, you will absolutely love this tropical tip of Texas. You will be able to rent just about anything you can think of to help you enjoy your days in the sun and surf, such as jet skis, waverunners, kayaks, and hobie cats. Windsurfing and kitesurfing are also very popular sports on the island, as are parasailing and sky diving. If this much adventure scares you, just don your prettiest suit, grab a towel and a good book, and enjoy the unforgettable beauty of the beach.

You can experience one of the newest, most exciting water attractions anywhere at the South Padre Island Schlitterbahn on Park Road Hwy 100. In the center of the Park you'll find Rio Adventure, an endless river that carries its tubed passengers through lazy waters into crazed speed rapids. It will transport you up water "roller coasters" that blast you uphill on jets of water, then down exciting drops. The five-story Sand Castle Cove is a water fun house complete with geysers, water slides and soft-foam water toys for little ones. Your kiddos won't let you leave the Island without a visit to this fun waterpark.

If you can get up early enough, you'll find the best saltwater fishing along the Texas Gulf Coast, and to avid anglers, the lure is irresistible. More than 60 different charter companies and fishing captains offer bay and deep-sea fishing trips that will afford you "bragging rights." At the end of the day, you can have your restaurant of choice cook your catch! Fishing the Laguna Madre will render Speckled Trout, Redfish, Flounder, Black Drum and Sheepshead. Offshore fishermen reel in Amberjack, Tuna, Ling, Red Snapper, Kingfish, Grouper and Sailfish. Fishing the surf is very different from bay fishing. There are three sandbars that run parallel to the beach, and between each sandbar is a channel. Keep a watchful eye for working birds or signs of baitfish. "Plugging the surf" can be very satisfying. Ask any fisherman. The thrill of the weight of a heavy fish on the end of the line while enjoying the sunrise over the Gulf can be worth more than all of the buried Island treasure!

THE NATURE OF THE ISLAND

Nature lovers will enjoy the 34 miles of ecologically unspoiled beaches and sand dunes along the Gulf of Mexico, and birding enthusiasts will have an opportunity to observe more than 300 species of birds, including many migratory and shorebirds. Some visitors say that they become "accidental birders" before they even set foot on the island. At the base of the Queen Isabella Causeway, you'll see Black Pelican, Egrets, Roseate Spoonbills, Plovers and all types of Herons. The fall months bring birds headed south for the winter, and the spring months bring the feathered visitors to the

Island on their way home. The Yellow-billed Loon, the first one ever sighted on the entire Gulf Coast, was spotted on the Island. Another significant sighting was the Brown Booby, which hasn't been seen on the Island since 1988. The beautiful Laguna Madre Nature Trail provides access to the Laguna Madre Bay for birders. This trail is locally known as the "birding boardwalk," which takes nature lovers over wetlands and around a fresh-water pond where they will see a variety of Rails, Soras, Kingfishers, Moorhens, and many other species. Set up your birding scope at the "Warbler Rest Area," where Warblers, Tanagers, Orioles, Buntings and butterflies are known to rest on their trip to and from Central and South America. The wheelchair accessible Nature Trail is located next to the South Padre Island Convention Center and is free of charge.

Another incredible treat from nature is seeing the lively, friendly dolphins that entertain island visitors. Families of Bottlenose Dolphins live in the rich waters of the Laguna Madre Bay, and play in the waters near the shore. The dolphins are wild and free and can be seen all year long. A husband and wife team, George and Scarlet Colley, have been filming and documenting the island's dolphin families for seven years. They have learned that these families of dolphins have been living here their entire lives, and now are raising their babies on the rich food sources of the island waters. You may rent a dolphin watch boat for a tour, or join the study team for a private tour, but remember that it is against the law to swim with, feed, or touch wild dolphins.

ISLAND ACTIVITIES

One way to scoot to and from the many island attractions is "The Wave." The Wave is the island's trolley system, and makes stops at attractions, shopping areas, and many of the island's resort complexes and condominiums.

One of the biggest events of the summer is the Texas International Fishing Tournament, which takes place during July and August. For more than 65 years, this tournament has created an atmosphere of friendly fishing competition and great family fun. This five-day fishing event registers more than 1,400 anglers of all ages, and includes bay and offshore fishing. For information or registration, call 956-943-8438, or visit www.tift.org online.

Lady Anglers, bait your hooks! The Ladies Kingfish

Tournament has been an island tradition for more than 21 years, with winners bringing in Redfish, Trout, Flounder, Blackfin tuna, Bonito, Dorado and Kingfish. This tradition began long ago when several local ladies wanted their own tournament (after spending years traveling with their husbands to tournaments.) The first one was called, "The Yellow Rose of Texas," with only 20 anglers fishing in the offshore only tournament. Today, you see mothers and daughters and grandmothers and granddaughters fishing together, becoming a part of another great Texas tradition. E-mail the Chamber of Commerce for information, at info@spichamber.com.

PORT ISABEL

It has been called the "boating and fishing capital of tropical Texas," where refreshing breezes from the Gulf of Mexico meet the shores of historic Port Isabel. This gentle, seaside community is only 20 miles from exotic Mexico, and close to the beautiful shores of South Padre Island, making it a favorite place for vacationers and winter Texans. Boating and fishing are great any time of the year, whether you bring your own boat or rent a craft from one of the many marinas. You will experience the enchantment of bay life as you fish from the pier, or wade into the sparkling waters.

Into wildlife? You'll love watching the many Pelicans, Egrets, Roseate Spoonbills and migrating species, as well as delight in observing the friendly, dancing dolphins in the Laguna Madre Bay. At day's end, settle onto the deck of some of the city's most memorable restaurants for some delicious seafood. You will find everything from very casual to elite dining with marvelous menus featuring fresh seafood, steaks, prime rib, and Mexican dishes. Port Isabel offers everything for a wonderful visit—beautiful accommodations; full service boat-yards and marinas; RV parks; golf courses; restaurants; and specialty shops.

BEACON OF LIGHT

The view from the historic Port Isabel Lighthouse extends to the Laguna Madre and beyond to the Gulf of Mexico. The lighthouse is located on the "Point" of the Laguna Madre, a strategic location instrumental in the early settlement of Port Isabel and its maritime history. During the early 1500s, Spain sent explorers to this area, which was inhabited by the Coahilitecan Indians; however, it remained inhospitable to the Europeans until the mid 1700s. A land grant was awarded to Dona Rosa Maria Hinojosa that included this settlement, but it wasn't until the 1830s that Don Rafael Garcia established El Fronton de Santa Isabel (Point Isabel) to become the base for the Port of Matamoros. The Point Isabel Lighthouse was illuminated in 1853 and remained in operation until 1905 when shipping traffic declined. Mr. and Mrs. Lon C. Hill, Jr., and the Port Isabel Realty Company donated the lighthouse and its additional buildings to the State of Texas in 1950 because of its historical significance. The tower was remodeled to provide easy access for visitors, and is presently the only one of 16 lighthouses along the Texas coast open for public enjoyment. Today, the Port Isabel Lighthouse Square has blossomed with shops, restaurants, and museums. You may spend the day climbing the historical monument for a breathtaking view, learning the history of the port city at the museum, or selecting a unique souvenir from the gift shop. The Lighthouse Keeper's Cottage, located on the grounds, houses a display of lighthouse-related historical items, as well as the Port Isabel Chamber of Commerce. This is open daily 9 a.m.–5 p.m.

HISTORICAL MUSEUMS

In addition to the Lighthouse Keeper's Cottage Museum, you will want to visit the fascinating Treasures of the Gulf Museum and the Port Isabel Historical Museum. The historic Champion Building, home of the Port Isabel Historical Museum was built in 1899 as a dry goods store and residence. It also once served as a post office and a railroad depot. The Port Isabel Historical Museum has much to offer. It houses two levels, a theater, a gift shop, and one of the largest collections of Mexican artifacts from the U.S.-Mexican War. It also is known for the remarkable fish mural, painted by a local fisherman in 1906. The Treasures of the Gulf Museum located next to the historical museum features displays that tell the story of the three Spanish ships which wrecked off the northern end of South Padre Island in 1554—just 30 miles north of Port Isabel. Inside, you'll find a Children's Discovery Lab, offering hands-on exhibits of marine archeology. Kids love the "ship theater" and nautical-inspired gift shop.

GREAT FISH TALES

Ahoy, Landlubbers! Professional and friendly crews will assist you on board one of the many great charter boats that launch from Port Isabel. Certified by the U.S. Coast Guard, these companies offer deep-sea fishing; bay fishing; dolphin watching and marine ecology tours; fireworks cruises; and even sunset trips that will become lasting memories of your visit to Port Isabel. Many of these boats are air-conditioned and equipped with the latest technology. Some provide free rod, reel, bait, and tackle, as well as crew demonstrations on how to use the gear. Contact the Chamber of Commerce for a list of Charter Companies.

LOS FRESNOS

Neighboring Los Fresnos has both "city flavor" and "country charm." Here you can visit the world-famous Little Graceland Museum, or attend one of the authentic Texas-style rodeos. The prairie and coastal lands provide intriguing landscapes for birders, and the agricultural industry provides citrus fruits and watermelons all year long.

For more information on South Padre Island, call the South Padre Island Convention and Visitors Bureau at 800-SOPADRE or visit www.spichamber.com.

For more information on Port Isabel, call the Port Isabel Chamber of Commerce 800-527-6102 or visit www.portisabel.org.

South Padre Island / Port Isabel
Fairs Festivals & Fun

January
SPI Market Days
Taste of the Island and Trade
Show
Winter Texan Golf Classic
The Longest Causeway Run &
Wellness Walk

February
SPI Kite Fest
Port Isabel Winter Texan
Appreciation Day
SPI Chili Expo "SPICE"
Winter Texan 8-Ball
Championship

March
Spring Break

April
SPI Semana Santa
SPI Visitor Center Easter Egg
Hunt
Port Isabel's Founders
Celebration

May
SPI Windsurf Blowout
Rio Grande Valley Regional Red
Chili & Salsa Cook-off
Memorial Day Weekend
Fireworks Over the Bay
Memorial Weekend Volleyball
SPI Chamber Chili Cook-off
Taste of the Tropics (Port Isabel)

June
Cine Sol Latino Film Festival

July
Fourth of July Fireworks Over
the Bay
SPI Volleyball / Co-Ed Doubles
Beachcombers Art Show & Sale
Texas International Fishing
Tournament
Flow Rider Amateur Body
Boarding Competition

August
Ladies Kingfish Tournament
"Bandit Run" for Ruffriders
Labor Day Weekend Fireworks
Over the Bay
SPI Volleyball / Labor Day
Tournament
Flow Rider Summer Series
National Championship
Texas International Fishing
Tournament

October
Sand Castle Days
SPI Bikefest
Port Isabel Market Days

November
World Championship Shrimp
Cook-off
Tails of SPI Fun Fly Fiesta
Lighting of the Island

December
Island of Lights Holiday Parade
Christmas Street Parade
Port Isabel Lighted Boat Parade

Art, Artists, Art Galleries, Framing & Specialty Shops

Internationally-known wildlife artist Larry Haines has taken the two things he has loved since childhood and turned them into a very successful business venture. The Shop, at 318 Queen Isabella Blvd in Port Isabel, is an art gallery, custom frame shop, and fly-fishing outfitter. Larry has loved fly-fishing all of his life, and became interested in drawing and painting wildlife as a young child. His works have been featured in *Houston Audubon Society Magazine, Field & Stream, Marlin Magazine, and Florida Sportsman Magazine.* His paintings of coastal birds and wildlife, as well as South Texas landscapes, hang throughout the store, and Larry's wife Molly will custom build a beautiful frame for your print. Both original paintings and limited-edition prints are available. Avid fishermen will love the selection of custom fly-rods and fly-fishing gear. Open Tuesday-Saturday 9 am-5 pm and Sunday noon-3 pm. Call 956-943-1785.

"They look alike, they walk alike, at times they even talk alike!" They are sisters, Ann Hunsaker and Linda Golden, and they are the toast of the town. Many island visitors tell us that they won't leave until they've made a stop to say "hi" to the sisters. Ann and Linda have quite a following from locals and visitors alike who have heard of their beautiful and unique gift shop. "Sisters" located over the Queen Isabella Causeway at Plaza 410 Padre Blvd in South Padre Island, is a quaint shop that has been in business since 1986. Through the years, they have enlarged the store, and expanded its lines of original art, hand-crafted furniture, hand-painted pottery, and fun treasures for every room in the house. They are very proud to carry the beautiful line of Mackenzie-Childs pottery and enamelware. When the artist came for a day to sign her artwork, the response was so over-whelming that she ended up staying for three days.

Everything about the store is beautiful and fun. The soft aromas of soap crystals and candles, and the beautiful music create a wonderful shopping atmosphere. We loved the hand-made jewelry by local silversmith Shirley Christensen who tumbles her own stones and designs the exquisite original pieces.

The sisters consider themselves lucky because they absolutely love what they do, and they love that they can spend so much time with each other. When asked about the key to their success, Linda says, "We are two different people, with different strengths." We say they make a great team! Stop by and visit, shop, buy, and even take pictures in front of the black awning in front of the building, which reads "Sisters."

The shop is open Monday-Saturday 10 am-6 pm and Sunday noon-5 pm. Call 956-761-2896.

Kitty and Ralph Ayers met while he was an art student at Mexico City College in 1962, and they have been involved in the art world ever since. Their desire to create a local center for the arts led to the opening of the Purple Parrot Gallery and Gift Shop at 419 E. Maxan Street in Port Isabel. Here you'll find an eclectic collection of fine art and decorative art for every taste and pocketbook. They feature local and regional, Texan and Mexican artists. You'll also find handcrafted gifts, jewelry, toys, and collectibles from around the world. The gallery is open Monday-Saturday 10 am-6 pm and Sunday noon-5 pm. Call 956-943-2004.

Linda Whitby credits her talented artist mother, who escorted her to many museums and galleries, for her passion and love for beautiful art. Recognizing a specific need for a fine art gallery, and encouraged by the Island's artistic enthusiasm, she opened Art~Local & Beyond at 410 Padre Blvd in South Padre Island. The revues have been wonderful, and the gallery has become the "buzz" in art circles. Artists, collectors, and serious art patrons are excited and impressed with the fine art gallery.

Linda continuously mixes contemporary art with more traditional styles, and features the artwork of local artists as well as artists from across Texas, Mexico and beyond. And, she is constantly adding new artists to the roster. The gallery is open Monday-Saturday 10 am-6 pm and Sunday in the summer. For more information, call 956-761-9999 or visit www.art-spi.com.

Attractions & Entertainment

Now that's one big sandcastle! Sons of the Beach Sandcastle Wizards, who compete in sandcastle building contests throughout the world, created the incredible sandcastle—located at the center—and restore it regularly. It took more than 45 tons of sand mixed with about 50 pounds of clay and 200 gallons of water to build the 10-foot statue that welcomes visitors to the island. It's the biggest one in all of Texas!

The Convention Centre is located at 7355 Padre Blvd on the north end of South Padre Island. Built in 1992, this modern, airy, and colorful building was created to host a wide variety of events. It offers more than 75,000 square feet of meeting space, including the column-free 22,500 square foot exhibit hall as well as a conference theater for 300 and a spectacular view of the Laguna Madre Bay. One of the most beautiful sites to see at the Convention Centre is the famous "Whaling Wall #53" by acclaimed environmental artist Wyland. Wanting to show homage to whales and other creatures of the sea, Wyland devoted his talent to painting 100 walls across the world. The South Padre Island Convention Centre wall was his 53rd project. It is 153 feet long and 23 feet high. More than

2,000 Valley school children and hundreds of spectators were allowed to watch him work.

The Convention Centre is the perfect place to book a meeting, convention, concert, or special event. In fact, the 2002 Miss Teen USA Pageant was held here! The friendly staff at the center has one goal—to promote tourism and assist visitors while they are on the island. The Visitor Centre, 600 Padre Blvd, is open seven days a week 8 am-5 pm. Find out more by calling 956-761-3005 or visit www.sopadre.com. *(Color picture featured in front section of the book.)*

Most people wonder what it would be like to ride a beautiful horse across a white sandy beach, with the wind gently blowing their hair, and the water lapping softly at the heels of their steed. Yes, it is the idyllic Hollywood scene, yet it's possible, on South Padre Island. The Island Equestrian Center offers exciting horseback riding on the beach even to regular folks,

for all riding levels. Although guides accompany the group to give basic instruction, riders are given the opportunity to trot or lope the horses. Call, 956-761-4677 for group discounts and reservations or you can check out their schedule and rates by visiting www.horsesonthebeach.com.

Gifts, Home Décor
& Interior Design

ACCENTS

After retiring and traveling the country with her husband, Jane Langenheim is back to work, and we're so glad. One visit to her store, Accents, 201 W. Queen Isabella Blvd  in Port Isabel, and you'll be glad, too! It's a treasure trove of colorful lifelike silk arrangements, pillows, rugs, candles, kitchen and tabletop accessories. Transform your patio and garden with silk plants, trees, pottery, water fountains, steppingstones and wind chimes. Accents carries gifts for men, clocks, designer watches, jewelry and wall crosses. "Just for fun" gifts, flags, banners, windsocks and all the accessories for the young at heart. You'll love the Blue Mountain greeting cards and books, and the wonderful selection of fine local and international art. Accents offers gift wrapping and UPS delivery. Open Monday-Saturday 9 am-5:30 pm. Call Jane and Andrea at 956-943-7888.

CACTUS FLOWER INTERIORS

The comment Jeri Garrett hears most often from Island shoppers is, "We can't find anything like this at home!" Cactus Flowers Interiors at 3009 Padre Blvd in South Padre Island, is a beautiful gift and interiors boutique with a focus on "coastal living." Jeri carries unique items for the home or beach condo that capture the simple, casual feel of island life. Everything about the store is fresh and unique, from the clean, refreshing smell of scented candles and bath soaps to the very unique glassware and "island art." Opened by Jeri and her mother back in 1981, Cactus Flower Interiors has evolved through the years into one of the island's most well respected businesses. As a licensed interior designer, Jeri works with clients to create beautiful decors that compliment the emerald green waters and sugar white sands of the coast. There are two talented floral designers on staff who are well known for their work with coastal weddings. Cactus Flower Interiors will ship across the United States, and offers Teleflora services, too. The shop is open Monday-Saturday 10 am-6 pm. For information, visit www.cactus-flowerinteriors.com or call 956-761-7771.

 Artist and designer Brandi Reneé, along with her husband interior remodeling contractor John Day, have teamed up with their daughters to provide the island with a total design service. Together, this talented family opened Decora Design at 2500 Padre Blvd in South Padre Island—home decor and design center specializing in coastal bedding and island decor. Brandi has a full scale, on-site workroom in which she manufactures curtains, bedding and pillows for her clients and the store. If "coastal bedding" summons visions of luxurious comfort, incredible fabrics, and breezy colors, you have a good idea of what you'll find in this beautiful store. "Island decor" is portrayed in the unique gift items and home accessories like tropical potpourri, and exotic beaded and feathered lamps. Brandi is the designer for the South Texas division of U.S. Homes, and has fully furnished more than 12 model homes for the builders. Enjoy expert advice and Southern hospitality—cookies and tea—in this wonderful island store Monday-Saturday 10 am-6 pm and see how beautiful coastal living can be. Call 956-761-6776 to learn more.

Fashion, Accessories & Jewelry

The Silver Junction

Andrea Moses truly believes the saying, "Do what you love, and success will follow." She absolutely loves what she does, and The Silver Junction at 224 W. Ocean Blvd in Los Fresnos grows more popular and successful every year. She was working as an interior decorator until so many women began literally stopping her on the  street to ask about her unique silver jewelry. That's when she focused her creative energy in the fashion world, and opened The Silver Junction in 1996. Andrea says that she is supported by her

 husband, has God as her Chairman of the Board, and that every day is more fun than the last. Her store is a visual enticement of sterling silver designs with varying stones from around the globe. Hours are Monday-Saturday 10 am-6 pm. Call 956-233-1500.

SHIP SHAPE

Ship Shape, 5212 Padre Blvd in South Padre Island, is in the business of equipping people with all the essentials for the perfect day at the beach. If you're looking for cute short outfits, embroidered t-shirts, or any other kind of beachwear for men, women and children; the latest in surfer, beach style jewelry; or even a new addition to your home décor; chances are, you'll find it here!

Besides a Yorkie named Zak and Tuaca the kitty, this animal-friendly shop has a lot to offer that make it a local favorite. Locally-run-and-owned, Ship Shape will prepare you for your beach adventure. You can shop cross country too! Whether it's beach towels, clothes, a special gift or a decoration you're looking for, Ship Shape will help you find it—and ship it! With a conveniently-placed shipping company just next door, Ship Shape can ship any item, anywhere.

Open Monday-Saturday 9 am-9 pm and Sunday 9 am-6 pm. For more information, visit www.shipshapespi.com or call 956-761-2111.

BECKY'S PLACE

Armed with a marketing degree and a lifetime of watching her father run his own business, Becky Parce couldn't wait to get into the retail business. When she moved to South Padre Island in 1983, she opened a ladies retail shop specializing in clothing for women age 30 to 60. Because the island lends itself to a more casual way of life, her inventory reflects that feel. She maintains a reputation of having unique fashions that work well with the Valley lifestyle, yet are acceptable for travel to other places. Becky loves the challenge of going to market in various cities to find the right merchandise. You'll find lots of jewelry and accessories for that final touch, as well as shoes and handbags. Becky believes that colorful fun clothing makes a woman feel great, and her biggest reward is a satisfied customer. Visit Becky's at 1604 Padre Blvd. in South Padre Island, Monday-Saturday 10 am-6 pm and Sunday noon-5 pm. Call 956-761-4074.

Hotels, Motels, Condominiums & Realtors

Imagine being able to combine business and pleasure! That's what Lynne Tate did when she and her family moved to South Padre Island. After more than 35 years of being a frequent visitor to the Island, Lynne was able to merge her years of real estate experience with her love of the area. In 1994, she opened her real estate company on South Padre Island.

Lynne Tate Real Estate now has several fulltime agents with many combined years of experience. The friendly, professional staff strives to make every sale a positive experience and takes pride in the number of repeat customers and clients generated by their commitment to service, integrity and client satisfaction. Clientele includes buyers and sellers from the Rio Grande Valley, and from across the United States, Mexico and Canada. The company specializes in beach and bay side homes, as well as condominiums, commercial properties and undeveloped land in South Padre Island, Port Isabel, Laguna Vista, Bayview and the South Padre Island Golf Course.

Lynne Tate Real Estate is located at 2200 Padre Blvd, and is open Monday-Saturday 9 am-5 pm and Sunday noon-5 pm. For more information, call 956-761-1400, 888-646-6069 or visit www.southpadrerealestate.com online. *(Color picture featured in front section of the book.)*

ISLAND SERVICES

It's great to know that when you come to the island in need of a good place to stay, you can count on Bob and Maria Pinkerton at Island Services to find the perfect spot for your vacation in the sun! Island Services, located at 1700 Padre Blvd, is a property management, condominium rental, and real estate company for properties on  South Padre Island. It is a family-owned-and-operated business that has become a well-respected company over the last 30 years. Bob and his family know the island and its people, and they love the many tourists and "winter Texans" they've had the opportunity to help over the years. Whether you need a one, two, or three-bedroom condominium, or even just an efficiency apartment, they have many to show.

Bob Pinkerton served four years as Alderman, from 1982-1986, and as mayor of South Padre Island from 1986-1992. He had so much support and respect from the townspeople that he was asked to run again in 2002, and is presently serving a fourth term as the island's mayor. Maria Pinkerton is from Belize, in Central America, and is a partner in the business. This dynamic duo is well known and loved throughout the island. The Pinkertons love the area and feel they have their finger on the pulse of the community and the area real estate properties. This combination has made for a very successful business! They represent the owners of many condominiums and waterfront homes for lease or sale, so whether you are in need of a place for the weekend, a summer home for a few months, a place to call your own, Island Services should be your first stop. You'll find everything from small, cozy cottages to high-rise, ocean-front condos, in many price ranges. Visit the office for brochures and information on all of the rentals, seven days a week from 8 am-5 pm. For more information call 956-761-2649 or visit www.island-services.com.

QUALITY INN South Padre Island

Swish down the water slides at Schlitterbahn, bask in the South Padre Island sun, or stroll through the award-winning arts community. Then come to Quality Inn, where the memories are yours to keep! This brand-new South Padre Island inn offers a beautiful view of the bay from every room, which includes a mini-fridge, a safe, a coffee maker, and wireless Internet service. A Monterrey décor compliments the hand-carved uniqueness of every piece of furniture in the hotel, and the entire inn is filled with beautiful pieces of original art. The Bay View Room contains history and paintings by artist Richard Hall, featuring lighthouses of the South Padre Island and Port Isabel area from the last 150 years.

Whether you plan to fish, swim, sightsee, or shop, you'll start energized after the Quality Inns continental breakfast. This is served in the Bay View Room, overlooking the Queen Isabella causeway and the calm waters of the bay. Your family will also enjoy a fireworks display over the bay every Friday night from Memorial Day to Labor Day—without even leaving the hotel! You'll lose yourself in the crimson sunsets, and feel enveloped in this unique resort community. This luxurious, yet budget conscious hotel makes it possible for you to enjoy a memorable, affordable visit to the beautiful island. Seventy-five percent of the rooms are non-smoking, and choice privileges are offered in a frequent travler

program. One of the best perks—kids under 18 stay free. Keep an eye out for the Lighthouse on the top of the hotel at 901 Padre Blvd. For reservations, call 956-761-4884, or take a visual tour through www.qualityinn.com/hotel/tx557 online.

WHITE SANDS
MOTEL, MARINA AND RESTAURANT

You'll have everything you need at this popular Port Isabel all-in-one motel, marina and restaurant located at 418 W. Hwy 100. Patrick Marchan has operated this fishing and seafood business on the channel and has built an excellent reputation for great customer service since 1988.

A full-service marina offers boat slips for motel customers and restaurant guests, as they enjoy waterfront dining on the deck. There are motel units, which rent by the day, week, or month as well as two-bedroom apartments with a three-day minimum. Fishermen will find everything for a great catch including live and frozen bait, fish cleaning utensils, rod and reel rentals, a freezer for fish storage, tackle, gas and oil, snacks, beer, and a guide service if needed. They will even cook your "catch of the day!" Call White Sands Motel at 956-943-2414 or the Marina at 956-943-6161 or visit www.the-white-sands.com.

Restaurants

Yes, this place is as charming as its name suggests, and yes, you will see Bottlenose Dolphins compete for your attention. Dolphin Cove Oyster Bar is located right at the mouth of the jetties, at the southern tip of South Padre Island in Isla Blanca Park, overlooking the beautiful Brazos Santiago Pass. Dress casually and come with a big appetite. Mary Jo and "Joe Buck" Camp have been in business here for 14 years, and have gained a wonderful reputation throughout the Valley and the admiration of fans from across Texas who have voted Dolphin Cove "Best Peel & Eat Shrimp on the Island." It is open Tuesday-Sunday noon until … Visit www.spisland.com/dolphincove or call 956-761-2850.

They've hoisted the "Jolly Roger," manned the faux cannons, and emptied the nets from the fishing boats, to make sure your visit to Pirate's Landing is one you and your family will treasure. They will cook your catch of the day, or you can try something from their menu, which features fresh delicious seafood, burgers, and sides. Appetizers include seafood stuffed jalapenos, and boiled shrimp, with entrees of Cajun spiced redfish and stuffed shrimp. There are fajitas, delicious desserts, and a fun children's menu, too! The food is plentiful and delicious, and it is all made just about perfect by the beautiful bay view. Pirate's Landing is located at 110 N. Garcia at Lighthouse Square, and is open daily for lunch and dinner at 11:30 am. This is one of the most popular and fun restaurants in Port Isabel! For more information, visit www.searanchtx.com or call 956-943-3663. *(Color picture featured in front section of the book.)*

The Catch of the Day? The top-notch, top-rated Sea Ranch Restaurant is waterfront dining at its best! It is one of the oldest restaurants on the island, and is located at #1 Padre Blvd on South Padre Island. Take time before dinner to relax on Dirty Dave's Deck, enjoy a beautiful sunset with your margarita; and watch the fishing boats come in. The seafood is brought in daily by their own fleet of fishing and shrimp boats, so everything is very fresh. Just one bite of the grilled red snapper, or crunchy fried shrimp, and you'll agree with *Hospitality Magazine*, who has rated Sea Ranch Restaurant one of America's top 500 restaurants for the past five years. After dinner, make a wonderful evening unforgettable with drinks and music on Dirty Dave's Deck. You'll enjoy the lively entertainment, and get an earful of local chit chat. Open daily 4:30-10 pm. For more information, visit www.searanchtx.com or call 956-761-1314. *(Color picture featured in front section of the book.)*

"World Champion-Shrimp" dishes, Peanut Butter Shrimp and Shrimp Marco Antonio are just two of the delicious creations found at Scampi's Restaurant & Bar at 206 W. Aries Drive in South Padre Island. Renowned for these tasty creations, freshness and top-shelf quality, Scampi's is "the place" to watch the sunset.

You will enjoy the finest fresh fish and shellfish, including live lobster and Dungeness crab, as well as U.S.D.A. prime grade aged steaks and veal. The cuisine is an eclectic combination of Continental, Mediterranean, Asian, and Southwest, all served with fresh baked breads and unique dessert items. We simply loved it! Combine their fine food offerings with the perfect wine selection from their extensive list of wines from all parts of the world, for an incredibly romantic Bayside dining experience.

Scampi's Restaurant & Bar is open Monday-Thursday and Sunday 4:30-10 pm and Friday-Saturday until 11 pm. Enjoy wonderful island entertainment in the lounge—the unforgettable sunsets are complimentary! Call 956-761-1755.

PALMETTO INN

For many families who visit the Island annually, dining at Palmetto Inn is a treasured tradition. Three generations have enjoyed being part of the history of this family-owned Mexican restaurant, which is located at 1817 Padre Blvd. It is the oldest restaurant on South Padre, and is owned by Sam and Christy Carrasco. VIP's such as Presidents Lyndon B. Johnson, Ronald Reagan, and George W. Bush have visited them. You'll enjoy the freshest seafood; incredible, authentic Mexican food; and delicious homemade chips and salsa. Make it one of your favorite traditions! Opens daily at 11:30 am and closes at different times depending on the season. Call 956-761-4325.

WHITE SANDS RESTAURANT

Marchan's White Sands Restaurant at 418 W. Hwy 100 is a local Port Isabel favorite, and has been called, "extraordinary" in *Coastal Living* Magazine's article on "the best

seafood dives." Once you experience it, you'll understand why. Owner Patrick Marchan, was born and raised in Port Isabel, and is, in fact, the town's Mayor. He highly recommends everything on his menu, which includes wonderful delights from the sea—shrimp, oysters, crab, flounder, and lobster. We loved the blackened seafood! Marchan also offers a special service to his customers. He says, "you catch them, we'll cook them," and everything is served with the great sides like coleslaw, fries and sauces. White Sands Restaurant is open Monday 5 am-2 pm and Tuesday-Sunday 5 am - 9 pm. For more information, visit www.the-white-sands.com online or call 956-943-2414.

DISCOVER
ROMA / RIO GRANDE CITY

ROMA

WHERE IT ALL BEGAN

More than 100 years ago, oblate Fathers described Roma as one of the most compact and picturesque towns along the Rio Grande with only 1,000 inhabitants. Today, a century later, it is pretty much the same—a small, picturesque town of about 10,000 people. It has retained much of its original Old World charm and dignity, and many of its townspeople are descendants of the original pioneer families.

The history of Roma can actually be divided into two parts. The earliest history goes back to its 1765 founding by Spanish colonists who established ranches. Modern Roma dates back to the early 1840s when the settlement began to become a real village, much to the credit of the Rio Grande River. When Texas became a state, Roma was one of the first custom inspection stations, and by the 1900s Roma had become a trade center for people on both sides of the river.

Today, the town offers all of the advantages of small-town living with a quiet, slow pace of life in the midst of very friendly folks. Its close proximity to Falcon Lake and Falcon State Park make it ideal for tourists who love the outdoors, and because it is so close to Mexico, there are many business and tourism opportunities.

Historians and architects find the layout of Roma absolutely fascinating. Reflecting the Hispanic tradition of a plaza, the Town Square is lined with continuous structures, with a church as the focal point. And, all of the buildings have expansive courtyards designed in the Hispanic/Moorish tradition. Although the Town Square has seen hard times through the years, it has remained charming. Fame came to the tiny town in 1952, when Hollywood chose Roma's town square as the backdrop for the movie, "Viva Zapata," starring Marlon Brando, Anthony Quinn, and Jean Peters. The square is presently being renovated, and thanks to this restoration project, South Texas travelers can discern much of its original grace.

A BRIDGE TO THE PAST   (See Cover)

One of the city's most popular attractions is the 700-foot long Roma-Ciudad Miguel Aleman Steel Suspension Bridge. It was constructed during the 1920s and is the only remaining suspension bridge across the Rio Grande today. It was built on sandstone cliffs over the Rio Grande, and is considered to be one of the most striking, earlier 20th century bridges in Texas. Many winter Texans participate in an annual bike journey, which begins at Roma's National landmark district and crosses over to the Sister City of Ciudad Miguel Aleman.

It is said of this tiny Texas town, "With its architectural richness, Roma is ideal in the United States and Texas for interpreting the Hispanic lifeways of river towns and the borderland cultures." You can find out about the many sightseeing adventures and annual festivals by contacting the Roma Chamber of Commerce.

RIO GRANDE CITY

IN THE BEGINNING

The Starr County Seat sprang up around Roma and Fort Ringgold, and is one of the oldest communities in the Valley. Visitors to Rio Grande City may visit the beautifully restored La Borde House, the former Fort Ringgold, which is now home to the Rio Grande City Independent School District, and a replica of the Grotto of Lourdes in France.

Fort Ringgold has a rich history, dating back to 1848, as one of the chain of forts built as a defense adopted on the western frontier. It includes the Robert E. Lee House; the Officers' Quarters; the hospital; the guardhouse and bakery; and the army barracks.

The Borde House, which was originally built by Françoise La Borde and later renovated in 1982 by San Antonio businessman Larry Sheerin, once again offers travelers elegant rooms with authentic Creole, Victorian, and Texan charm.

Perhaps the most fascinating attraction of Rio Grande City is the Grotos of Lourdes, on the northeast corner of Brittan Avenue. This replica of the Grotto of Lourdes in France was built as nearly true to the original as possible, from rocks and petrified wood. The Loomis Studio in Paris, France, donated the statue of the Virgin Mary and the peasant girl, Bernadette Soubirous. The Grotto was dedicated in 1928.

It is said that in Rio Grande City, the line between past and present "gently fades." The town is rich in history, with pure South Texas heritage, and holds a charm all its own. The Texas Historical Commission designated Rio Grande City as an official Texas Main Street City in 2002. It is also part of Los Caminos del Rio, "roads of the river," a historic place rich in natural and cultural legacies. The townspeople are welcoming and gracious hosts, and make their visitors feel like royalty. Don't miss this charming town on your Lady's Day Out!

For more information on Roma, call the Roma Chamber of Commerce at 956-849-1411 or visit www.cityofroma.net.

For more information on Rio Grande City, call the Rio Grande City Chamber of Commerce at 956-487-3024 or visit www.riograndecity.com.

Roma / Rio Grande City
Fairs Festivals & Fun

March
> Starr County Youth Fair

June
> Farm & Ranch Expo & Rodeo (Rio Grande City)

July
> Fourth of July

October
> Vaquero Day Festival (Rio Grande City Main St.)
> Roma Fest

December
> Night Time Christmas Parade (Rio Grande City)

ROMA
ECONOMIC DEVELOPMENT CORPORATION

With its rich southwestern flavor and incredible architectural history, Roma may be one of Texas's best-kept secrets. Reflecting the Hispanic tradition of a plaza, the Town Square was designed in the Hispanic/Moorish tradition with a church as a focal point. The square was so charming that it served as the backdrop for the 1952 movie "Viva Zapata" starring Anthony Quinn and Marlon Brando.

Today, the Roma Economic Development Project is at the heart of a movement to renovate and restore the best of Roma's masterpieces. Which include the Ramirez Hospital, a colorful two-story structure once used as a quasi-military building and now as a hospital. The R. Garcia Ramirez House and Store, constructed in 1881 as a home for the Garcia Ramirez family and becoming a housing commercial enterprise in 1925. Also, renovated, the Antonia Saenz Building and adjacent courtyard, a one-story load-bearing brick masonry residential structure. In restoration are several non-historic buildings such as the Coffee Pot Building and the Plaza itself.

The 200-hundred-year-old walls of the visitor complex at 77 Convent Street offer an exciting trip through Roma's cultural history, and should be your first stop when visiting this beautiful town. The World Birding Center will be housed at the complex. For more information, contact the City of Roma at 956-849-1411 or visit www.cityofroma.net. *(Color picture featured on the front cover.)*

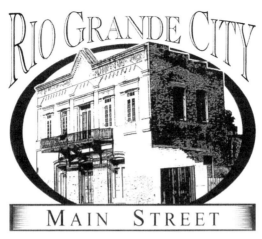

MAIN STREET

With an atmosphere that blends the Old West and Old Mexico, Rio Grande City's Main Street draws visitors from across the nation to enjoy the past and present of this historic border town. Main Street has the feel of the frontier of the Wild Wild West. The area was originally called Carnestolendas in 1768, but founded as Rio Grande City in 1846. Shortly after, Fort Ringgold was established as an army post for protection of U.S. citizens during the Mexican War, and other buildings began to spring up in what is today Main Street. The Siliverio de la Pena Building, built in 1886, and the La Borde House, in 1899 have been renovated to preserve the early history of the town. An application for a "Main Street Designation" was sent to the Texas Historic Commission and awarded to the city November 2001. It received a National Main Street Designation by the National Trust for Historic Preservation as well.

The Rio Grande City Main Street Program is a community-based program whose purpose is to encourage all people to participate in the economic development of the downtown district. The Rio Grande Valley Main Street Program is housed in a group of buildings at 408 E. Main Street that are all part of the city's early days. Some of them were built during the mid 1800s and some even earlier, dating to its original settlement in the early 1700s. The program has been very successful in promoting the restoration, beautification, and economic development in this charming Texas town. Be sure to visit www.riograndecity.net for more information, and look for the upcoming eDowntownRio site, which will include listings of businesses in the Main Street district. Call 956-488-0047.

Gifts, Home Décor,
Health, Beauty
& Jewelry

Joyeria Daisy

This family-owned-and-operated jewelry store has been known for its beautiful jewelry creations and great personal service since 1975. Husband and wife Artemio and Maria Garcia specialize in custom designed earrings, bracelets, rings, and necklaces. Joyeria Daisy at 1651 E. Hwy 83 in Rio Grande City also offer jewelry repair, and guarantee their work. Hours are Monday-Friday 9 am-6 pm. For more information, call 956-487-1173.

℞ LINO'S PHARMACY ℞

After working for another pharmacy for many years, Lino Perez III decided that he wanted to have his own business. With lots of hard work, family support, and fierce determination, he opened Lino's Pharmacy at 708 Grant Street, and has been successful for more than 25 years.

The people of Roma and surrounding areas have come to know and respect the advice and service they receive from Lino, especially in the area of "personalized prescription information." Customers have confidence in Lino's advice and expertise. You'll trust him, too. Along with all of your prescription and over-the-counter drugs, you'll find jewelry, fine gifts, and accessories for the home—tucked into every nook at Lino's. Hours at Lino's Pharmacy are Monday-Friday 8 am-7 pm and Saturday 8:30 am-5 pm. Call 956-849-1811.

Hotels

LA BORDE HOUSE

La Borde House not only offers a great night's sleep, but also an unforgettable piece of history. Located in an officially named historical building, La Borde House, 601 E. Main Street in Rio Grande City, is an 1899 building restored to perfection. History buffs will love it!

Part of the Main Street's Revival Project, the hotel was restored with all its original authenticity—even down to its Victorian style gingerbread trim and wooden stair balusters.

La Borde House's beauty continues inside with furniture matching the hotel's initial period. With an inviting parlor, an elegant in-house restaurant and rooms ranging from historical, modern and even "grand bedrooms," La Borde House offers a touch of history and style that is missing in some of today's more modern hotels. Open everyday 8 am-9 pm. For more information or reservations, call 956-487-5101.

Restaurants & Bakeries

RB'S DINER

Established in 1985 right outside historic Roma, RB's Diner is considered by many to be the "Star of Starr County," when it comes to great traditional Tex-Mex food. Owned by the RB Escobar family, this family-owned, family-operated, and family-friendly restaurant, 4897 E. Hwy 83 in Roma, is proud to serve Starr County and the Lower Rio Grande Valley and welcomes visitors seven days a week for breakfast, lunch and dinner. Their specialties include the famous Tejano Bacon/Avocado Cheeseburger and RB's Fajita Botana Platter. Many patrons frequent the eatery daily for the delicious variety of Tejano and American special platters. Everything is homemade and very fresh. In fact, the flour tortillas are made by hand daily. They are delicious! RB's Diner is open Monday-Saturday 7 am-10 pm and Sunday 8 am-10 pm. You will love eating at RB's, where every customer feels like "family." Call 956-849-2156.

THE CAKE SHOPPE

You can't miss it! The huge sign outside boasts, "The Cake Shoppe, Home of the Carrot Cake." We had been told that Ludivina Garcia made the best carrot cake in Star County, so we sampled some. Girls—she does! She also makes quite a few other sweet creations that you really must try, but she's most famous for her deliciously moist carrot cake.

She began making them for birthdays for family and friends, and soon outgrew her home kitchen. She has been in the bakery business since 1976, and has quite a reputation for her delicious and beautiful cakes. Other specialties of Ludivina's are the Mexican Wedding Cookies, and multi-layered cakes for Quincineras. Stop by The Cake Shoppe at 4194 W. Hwy 83 in Rosita Monday-Saturday 6 am-6 pm or Sunday 10 am-3 pm. If you have a sweet tooth, you may never want to leave! Call 956 849-4883.

With three generations of bakers, it's no wonder El Valle Bakery is such a local hot spot. This family owned bakery has perfected its secrets of authentic Mexican pastries by passing them down through three generations. El Valle Bakery, 711 E. Main in Rio Grande City, has acquired quite a following in its 40 years of business. And, they've had to work hard to keep their secret family recipes a secret. Everyone wants to know!

Offering mouth-watering specialties such as Mexican sweet bread and authentic empanadas, they also make a point to honor cultural holidays with bread pudding for the Lent holidays and specialty bread made for days of importance such as the Day of the Dead and Three Wise Men days.

For a taste of perfected culture visit El Valle Monday-Saturday 6:30 am-7 pm and Sunday 7 am-2 pm. For more information, call 956-487-7430.

WONDERFUL WESLACO!

Staking his claim on a promising future, W. E. Stewart chose a portion of the former Llano Grande Land grant for the new town of Weslaco. The name was an acronym for W.E.Stewart Land Company. During this time in history, land companies were buying large tracts of land, cutting roads, and auctioning landsites to early settlers. The first site in Weslaco was sold in 1919, and the new town was off and running. Excursion parties from Chicago, Kansas City, and the Midwest brought settlers determined to convert wild brush into thriving agricultural land irrigated by pump stations and canal systems. The 1920s ushered in both incredible growth and natural disasters. The city experienced a devastating flood in 1923 and a fire that nearly destroyed the newly-established business district, but the community was only strengthened by these disasters. Weslaco began to rebuild relocating its business center to Texas Boulevard, which is the city's main street today.

Years have come and gone, but the enthusiasm of Weslaco's first settlers and business people remains. And, Weslaco shows no signs of slowing down. Its geography, available labor force, and exciting pro-business attitude make it ideal for distribution or retail businesses, and a focal point for Valley nature tourism. This vibrant Valley city offers a quality of life that includes excellent public and private schools; a community college; museums; theaters; a championship golf course; an airport; and great shopping opportunities. (We'll tell you all about these!) The plans for expansion are evident in its thriving, attractive downtown area, and in the can-do attitude of the local residents.

Weslaco is located on U.S. Expressway 83, 15 miles west of Harlingen, 15 miles east of McAllen, and only an hour's drive from

South Padre Island. You'll find the quaint little Mexico town of Nuevo Progreso just seven miles down the road, filled with street shops, curios, and arts and crafts. Weslaco is the heart of the Rio Grande Valley, welcoming visitors with a warmth and friendliness that says, "Give us a try and you, too, will discover what makes Weslaco wonderful!"

SHOPPING AND DINING IN WESLACO

Palm trees line Weslaco's Main Street, offering a welcoming entry to the city's unique shopping experiences. With a collective vision for their historical district, merchants have assembled a memorable shopping adventure. The 1930's Spanish colonial architecture has been kept intact throughout Main Street, and is reflective of the friendly hospitality of the city. You'll find a myriad of antique, clothing, jewelry, art, and home décor shops, and plenty to keep the husbands and kiddos amused while you shop!

You will relish the idea of dining in Weslaco, whether it is for a delicious, authentic, Mexican breakfast or lunch; a Texas barbecue; or something more international like Mediterranean, Italian, or continental cuisine. There is something for everyone!

FOR THE BIRDS!

Located in the heart of the verdant Rio Grande Valley, Weslaco is a favorite place for nature lovers. Its natural landscaping and abundance of native trees makes it a perfect location for bird and butterfly lovers from around the world. As part of the Great Texas Coastal Birding Trail, the spectacular viewing couldn't be better. Birders will find four sites on the trail surrounding the city, including the Weslaco Settling Ponds, the Valley Center, the Frontera Audubon Society, and the Llano Grande lake area. Get your binoculars ready—you might just catch a glimpse of the beautiful Green Jay, the Altamita Oriole, or even the Great Kiskadee. You'll find more beautiful birds in once place than anywhere in the United States—Weslaco is a great "birding headquarters!"

THE BEAUTIFUL REDHEADS!

Have a rendezvous with a beautiful redhead—parrot that is! One of the most fascinating events in Weslaco takes place about 20 minutes before sundown during the fall, winter, and early spring. You'll hear them coming before you see them—cries of "cleeoo, cleeoo, followed by ahk-ahk-ahk." Get ready, the redheads are here! Somewhere between 45 and 50 red crowned parrots (Amazona viridegenalis) have been living in the lower Rio Grande Valley for the past 100 years, and roost for the night around Weslaco's City Hall. The noise is incredible—chattering, squawking, screaming, and tilling. They are bright green in color with a red crown on the body, and a red wing patch. Once in a while, a blonde—er, uh a yellow-headed parrot may join the flock. The best place to observe the colorful, noisy, phenomenon of nature is to arrive at the intersection of 11th and South Kansas about an hour before sunset. Once the flock is situated, stay quiet and very still under the cover of the trees.

During the spring and summer, you may also see flocks of the Mexican green parakeets (Aratinga holochlora) flying over the Audubon Center and the City Cemetery. Remember that these species are protected by City Ordinance, and it is illegal to harm them in any way.

CITY ATTRACTIONS!

- Weslaco Main Street – It's a village of shops, restaurants, and specialty stores.
- Weslaco's historical Villa de Cortez Hotel has been completely restored and renovated into a bustling business, dining and shopping center.
- Valley Nature Center – Nestled in a beautiful part of Weslaco, this center offers a wonderful setting for learning about nature. Both the five-acre thicket of native vegetation and the paved self-guided trail offer good birding and excellent butterfly viewing year round.
- Frontera Audubon Center – Fifteen acres of dense thicket, sabal palms, marshes and lakes with trails for visitors to see migratory ducks, native birds, wild parrots, and colorful warbles. The Audubon Center has been home to the rare blue mockingbird and raucous parrots roosting for the evening. The Center is a model of how a city and a forest can coexist.
- Weslaco City Cemetery – Excellent birding all year, especially in the morning along the west edge of the drainage ditch on the east.

- Golden Raintree Citrus Garden – Beautifully landscaped gardens and ponds open to the public from November through March for birding.

- Tierra Santa Golf Course – Rated by *Golf Digest* as one of the best in the country, it is South Texas' most demanding golf course.

- Tower Theatre – Salvaged from an obsolete water storage container, this water tower landmark provides a unique space for artistic expression through theater productions.

- Bicultural Museum – Located next to the Weslaco Public Library, and across from City Hall, this museum tells the story of the blossoming community moving through time.

For more information on Weslaco, call the Weslaco Chamber of Commerce at 956-968-2102 or visit www.weslaco.com.

Weslaco
Fairs Festivals & Fun

February
    South Texas Music Festival

March
    Weslaco Appreciates Winter Texans
    Dia Del Tourista

April
    Texas Rio Grande Valley "Onion Festival"

May
    Cinco de Mayo
    Dragonfly Days

June
    Weslaco Roadrunner Night
    Toys For Big Boys

November
    Fiesta Market Day (Main Street)

December
    Annual Lighted Christmas Parade

Antiques, Gifts,
Home Décor & Tearooms

PIGEON HOUSE

The lovely antique shop and tearoom called "Pigeon House" was a life-long dream for sisters Belinda Turner and Andrea Jalufka. The unusual name for this beautiful place was taken from the book, *The Awakening* by Kate Chopin, in which the heroine makes a retreat for herself where she is surrounded by all of the things she treasures. Once inside, you'll agree that the name is fitting. In 1924, Newell Waters—a prominent architect—built the Pigeon House, 723 E. Hwy 83, for his new bride. Today, the house is home to lovely antiques; gifts for the home and bath; and an inviting tearoom where you'll be surrounded by the treasures of Pigeon House. You'll find NDI silk flowers; Lady Primrose products; and collectible Arthur Court pewter ware. The back windows of the tearoom reveal a courtyard full of beautiful tropical flowering shrubs, trees and plants. The atmosphere is lovely, and the food is delicious. Enjoy their refreshing signature "peach tea," with a slice of warm banana bread, and feast on homcmade soups, fresh salads, sandwiches, quiche, and, of course, dessert. Pigeon House is open Tuesday-Saturday 10 am-4 pm, serving lunch from 11 am-2 pm. Call 956-973-8577.

It is affectionately known as "The Little Shop That Got Way Out Of Hand!" Patti Dittburner was on the Main Street Board when she opened Bugambilias at 259 S. Texas Blvd. She wanted to be a mentor to "wanna be shop owners" who shared her desire to see Weslaco grow and thrive—mission accomplished. There are now 36 vendors offering a variety of items, including: antique and repro-duction furniture, jewelry, paintings, bath and kitchen items, Peruvian imports, bronze statues, Mexican Folk Art and a garden district. Great selection, great people, great fun! Hours are Monday-Saturday 10 am-6 pm and Sunday 1-5 pm. Call 956-447-0099.

MIMI'S ATTIC

Browsing through Mimi's Attic at 415 S. Texas Blvd in Weslaco is truly a little like poking around in grandmother's attic—minus the dust. You will find treasures tucked in every corner. This is a collection of more than 30 vendors who have put together the most amazing displays of antiques, and not quite antiques—everything from candles to cradles, lamps to antique linens. Look for the rus-tic cabinets and whimsical birdhouses outside welcoming visitors to this antique Mecca. Enjoy a cup of gourmet coffee with the owner and vendors, learn the history of their business; and buy the treasure you can't seem to put down. Hours are 9:30 am-6 pm Monday-Saturday. Call 956-968-6396.

Weslaco
Bicultural Museum

Preserving the treasured past for future generations...

The fascinating Weslaco Bicultural Museum was chartered in 1971, and takes pride in presenting the bicultural nature of Weslaco, honoring both Anglo and Hispanic pioneers of the community. You'll be able to traipse through Weslaco's history as you take in the permanent exhibits. The docents thrill you with personal stories about the exhibits, making you feel as though you were there!

Weslaco is the hometown of Harlon Block, one of the flag raisers of Iwo Jima, during WWII. The U.S. Marine Corp and the U.S. Weslaco Post Office donated a large wall size painting to the museum showing the flag rising.

See an early switchboard system used until 1929 in the valley. Stand next to a bed "Ty" Moulton Cobb, slept in, quilts dating back as far as the 1800s. The First National Bank once used the early bank safe that you'll see on display in the Guaranty State Bank exhibit and there are also many pictures of the town, its founders, and citizens dating back to Weslaco's beginnings in 1919. One of the most fascinating stories however, is the one of the town's birthday celebration, in which people actually made clothes for a style show from fresh fruits and vegetables grown in the Valley. You have to see the pictures to believe!

The Weslaco Bicultural Museum is located at 515 S. Kansas Avenue, and is open Wednesday-Friday 10 am-noon and 1 pm-4 pm and Saturday 10 am-4 pm. Programs are offered on a wide variety of topics. Call 956-968-9142 for more details.

Valley Nature Center

W   E   S   L   A   C   O

*A Secret Garden in the Heart of the
Rio Grande Valley*

Stroll through beautiful butterfly gardens, enjoy the reflective solitude of an elevated lily pond, and learn about the many native plants and wildlife of the Rio Grande Valley. The Valley Nature Center at 301 S. Border Avenue in Weslaco has it all! Their mission? "To provide education about the unique South Texas ecosystem to the Valley Community."

Their facilities house exhibits that focus on native flora and fauna specific to the Valley; a theater/conference room; and a wonderful gift shop. The Nature Park itself is a 5- acre wildscape with labeled native plants, and wildlife, including: birds, reptiles, tortoises, and butterflies. The first Saturday of each month you can join a "Butterfly Walk"—a guided tour throughout the park to enhance your identification skills. The second Saturday of each month, join the instructors and guides on a "Native Plant Walk," learning about the Valley's native plants and habitats. The third Saturday of each month is our favorite—a "Beginner's Bird Walk, getting tips on equipment, clothing, identification of birds, birding locations, ethics, and helpful resources. If you happen to be visiting Weslaco during the month of May, you'll be just in time for the fourth Annual "Dragonfly Days Festival" with field trips, presentations, kids activities and a keynote banquet. Such fun!

The Valley Nature Center is the perfect place for school field trips, which are offered Tuesday-Friday 9 am-12 pm or 1-3 pm. This program includes a short video and/or presentation, a guided nature walk in the urban park, and a knowledge hunt in the exhibit hall. The experts on hand emphasize wildlife and their habitat, explaining the fragile balance between them. You will love Saturdays in the Park. They are fun, educational, and memorable for the entire family. For more information, call 956-969-2475 or visit www.valleynaturecenter.org.

A performance at the Tower Theatre of Weslaco is more than just a theatre in the round. It is an exciting experience in a Texas Historical Building—a ground level water storage reservoir which was constructed in 1928. In the 1940s, a larger water tower was built next to the old one, and the old one was used for city storage. It wasn't until 1962, that City Manager, Cecil E. Massey had the vision to turn the old round eyesore into a community theatre. In 1969, Massey, his wife Mary Ann, and several others, established a theatre group, The Mid Valley Civic Theatre. Massey collected odds and ends, construction materials from builders, and even a light from a battleship, to create the first a theatre in the round in South Texas. The Mid Valley Civic Theatre has been working in partnership with the City of Weslaco to present theatrical productions at the Tower Theatre of Weslaco ever since.

The first performance at the Tower Theatre at 120 S. Kansas Avenue was held on April 2, 1970, and has since been home to hundreds of productions. Of course, through the years the threatre has been updated with a professional lighting system, air conditioning, risers for seating, and acoustical improvements, but the intimacy of the place and the enthusiasm of the actors have remained the same. Because of limited seating, it is important to make reservations.

Shirley Atkins is the only remaining board member of the original theatre board. She has directed or participated in all of the Theatre's 34 years of productions. Her daughter, Rise Morris, has been participating in shows since she was 6. The mother/daughter team have been directing musicals, plays, and children's shows for the last 21 years.

For information on upcoming presentations or to arrange tours of the facility, call 956-969-2368.

With its dense thicket, two ponds, a marsh, Sabal Palm forest and Citrus grove, this semi-tropical historical habitat located on the "twilight zone" is a magnet to resident and migratory birds from both the United States and Mexico. Weslaco has black-bellied whistling ducks, vireos, Incqa doves, green kingfishers, green jays, kiskadees, chachalacas, orioles, warblers, a large flock of red-crowned parrots, a rare blue mockingbird, and one of the best collections of butterflies in the area. The lush 15-acre urban tract has one mile of native habitat preserve, a wetlands flood control area, and is also the site of a large 1927 historical Spanish colonial revival residence and citrus grove.

In 1992, Bebe Skaggs James, whose parents were bankers and pioneer citrus growers, donated property to Frontera Audubon, a private, non-profit organization dedicated to the conservation and protection of the environment, wildlife and native habitat of the Texas lower Rio Grande Valley. Now, more than 10 years later thousands of visitors have "journey through time," taking a historical glimpse of the late 1920s in South Texas along the Mexican border. Two acres of grapefruit and orange trees are being planted adjacent to the house. These trees will produce varieties of fruit found in the late 1920s making the feel of the area even more authentic. The hacienda is planned to open as a historical living museum in 2005. At the far reaches of the habitat, you can see a beautiful historical bicultural city cemetery on land donated by the Skaggs.

The Frontera Audubon Museum and Thicket located at 1101 S. Texas Blvd in Weslaco is open Sunday-Friday 8 am-4 pm and Saturday 7 am-7 pm. Educational and special tours may be scheduled by visiting www.fronteraaudubon.org online or by calling 956-968-3275.

Fashion, Accessories &
Children's Shops

Look no further than Lionel's Western Wear for the finest western clothing, ladies boutique, and sterling silver jewelry. It's a downtown Weslaco tradition at 332 S. Texas Blvd that you don't want to miss! Lionel Sr. established Lionel's Western Wear in 1959, offering the best in western apparel and customer service. Today, it's the second generation, Sandy and Lionel Jr., who carry on the tradition. At Lionel's—you have the homey feel of a family-owned business. You'll not only leave with a beautiful new outfit, but also you will have made new friends.

Lionel's is a complete western wear store for men, women and children, plus a ladies boutique like no other! You'll love shopping at Lionel's, and you'll especially enjoy the old-fashioned, friendly service. Store hours are Monday-Saturday 9 am-6 pm. For more information, call 956-968-2552 or toll free at 877-968-2552.

THE STORYBOOK GARDEN & CELESTIAL BABY

Please do *not* miss this charming and beautiful children's bookstore at 260 S. Texas Blvd, Suite 106. It is a true Weslaco treasure! Sarah Cuadra opened The Storybook Garden with a desire to introduce young minds to literature, and provide lots of fun along the way. From the dress-up tea parties for children to story time at 11 am and 2 pm, children and adults alike enjoy the opportunity to learn, imagine, and dream. The store's motto says it best, " Books, gifts, & toys for growing minds." Sarah has also opened Celestial Baby, adjoining the bookstore, with "oodles of goodies for baby." Open Monday-Saturday 10 am-6 pm. For information, call 956-968-READ or 877-447-BABY.

Gardens, Orchards
& Produce

GOLDEN RAINTREE CITRUS GARDENS

The rich fertile soil, long warm days, and an abundant supply of water make the Rio Grande Valley conducive to growing the finest citrus in the world. Joe and Maryellen Harren have more than 100 acres of the Valley planted in citrus, and consider their Navel oranges and Rio Red grapefruit the "best of the best!" Together, he and Maryellen have built a very successful business, shipping fruit and gift baskets throughout the United States.

Choose from Ruby Red or Rio Red grapefruit, Navel, Marrs, or Valencia oranges, lemons and tangerines, as well as pecans, honey and delicious pralines. Visit the beautiful Golden Raintree Citrus Gardens at 1303 S. Texas in Weslaco to sample the goodies and explore the beautifully landscaped gardens. Hours are Monday-Saturday 9 am-6 pm during fruit season. Call 956-968-6161 or visit www.goldenraintreegardens.com.

Hotels

You can expect more than just a good night's sleep at the Fairfield Inn & Suites, 1005 Fairfield Blvd. You can expect to find friendly service; clean, comfortable rooms; and great features and amenities— all at very reasonable rates. The Fairfield-Weslaco has been named "Best in the USA," and General Manager Diane Moore has been awarded "National General Manager of the Year!" Diane is an energetic and motivated manager, and the entire staff is dedicated to making your stay a wonderful experience. Rooms have 25-inch TVs, cable, and well-lit work desks. The hotel also offers a dry cleaning service, a 24-hour fax and a copy service, a 24-hour coffee service, guest laundry, an exercise room, and an outdoor pool. Guests are also treated to a complimentary breakfast.

The inn is so nice you won't want to leave, but in case you do decide to roam—you'll be close to several attractions. You'll only be seven miles from great Mexican shopping and dining, and two miles from the Tierra Santa Golf Course. For more information or reservations, visit www.fairfieldinn.com online or call 956-968-6700, or 800-228-2800.

BEST WESTERN PALM AIRE HOTEL & SUITES

Best Western Palm Aire Hotel and Suites, 415 S. International Blvd is located in the heart of the semi-tropical Rio Grande Valley on US Expwy 83 and FM 1015 in Weslaco. Old Mexico-Nuevo Progreso and its markets and fine dining are just five miles away. Also, some of the world's best birding is right off of the property at the nearby Santa Ana Wildlife Refuge or many other nearby locations on The Great Texas Coastal Birding Trail. The lodgings are set in a lush tropical landscaped setting—a true resort ambience. Best Western offers tastefully appointed guestrooms, including suites, and the facilities also include the Courtyard Steakhouse Restaurant and Palm Aire Lounge, along with banquet and meeting space for up to 500 people. Guests enjoy three outdoor pools, health club, steam room, dry sauna, hot and cold spas, indoor racquetball courts, shuffleboard and lighted tennis court. Call 800-248-6511, 956-969-2411 or visit www.bestwesternpalmaire.com.

Interior Design & Builders

WESTGATE BUILDING CO.

Pablo Peña Jr. learned his trade as a young teenager, working alongside uncles as they built thousands of homes in the Houston area. He built his first home in Weslaco in 1954, and the rest is history. With the motto, "Experience has no Expiration Date," and 4500 homes under his "tool belt," Peña has gained the reputation as one of the finest homebuilders in the Valley. His high quality of work, fine craftsmanship, professional ethics, and outstanding reputation are what have made Westgate Building Company, 1400 N. Westgate Drive, a first choice for home builders in Weslaco. For more information, call 956-778-8686.

Restaurants & Bakeries

God has truly blessed this family business—from its humble beginnings 30 years ago to the successful bakery and tamale shop it is today. The Ibarras immigrated to this country from Mexico, and Mr. Ibarra learned the restaurant business from the "kitchen sink up." When his children, Maria and Martin Ibarra took over the restaurant, they decided to concentrate on cakes, bakery items and tamales. Weslaco residents are so glad!

Faithful customers count on them for the most delicious and beautiful cakes in all sizes and shapes, and the best tamales in town. Known for its creative cake designs, Ybarra's is a first choice for birthday, anniversary, and quinceañera celebrations, and of course, weddings. Visit Ybarra's Cake Shop and Bakery at 600 W. Railroad in Weslaco Monday-Saturday 7 am-7 pm. Call 956-968-9421 or visit online at www.ybarrascake.com or www.tamalesybarra.com.

JOSE'S CAFECITO

If the streets of Weslaco look a little empty on Saturday and Sunday mornings, it's because just about everyone is having breakfast together at Jose's Cafecito, 260 S. Texas Blvd. The restaurant is beautiful and multi-colored tiles add colorful charm to the historic building. Owners Tony and Janie Jasso claim to have the "best breakfast and Mexican food in town!" Looks like everyone agrees. We walked in as strangers, and left feeling like we were family. You'll love the delicious food, cozy atmosphere, friendly service, and of course, the very reasonable prices. Hours are Monday-Saturday 7 am-9 pm and Sunday 7 am-2 pm. Call 956-968-5057.

THE BLUE ONION

Be sure and check out this great restaurant in Weslaco, The Blue Onion at 2017 W. Expwy. See page 86 for full details.

Salons & Spas

new dimension

The first thing Elva Alanis will tell you about her exciting business is that it was God's answer to her prayers—He has allowed her to fulfill her dream! Elva came to the United States in 1985; began working; got married; became a Cosmetologist; and learned the beauty salon business from the ground up. Finally after 12 years of planning, saving, and dreaming, Elva was able to build and open her own shop. New Dimension Beauty Center held its grand opening in November of 2002 at 110 E. Agostadero Street in Weslaco. Her services include facials, nails, pedicures, manicures, haircuts, perms and highlights. You'll feel like a new person! The salon is open Tuesday, Wednesday and Friday 9 am-6 pm, Thursday until the last customer, and Saturday 8 am-4 pm. Call 956-969-4766.

Body & Soul Therapeutic Massage

Lifelong friends Lila Jones and Sherry Ballard both pursued nursing degrees and then expanded their knowledge in massage therapy. They opened their business, Body and Soul Therapy, desiring to see their patients receive immediate benefits that would make them feel great and enjoy a pain free life. Their compassionate and caring attitudes are evident in how they run their business, and are responsible for its wonderful success.

They offer massages, as well as a salt glow exfoliating treatment. Their beautiful new building is located at 110 E. Agostadero in Weslaco and is equipped with shower facilities for clients, making work-day treatments doable. Hours are 10 am-6 pm, Tuesday-Friday, by appointment on Saturday. Call 956-447-1336.

DISCOVER
RAYMONDVILLE / PORT MANSFIELD

Nature lovers young and old will find a little of everything wild in Willacy. From the ranch lands to the coastal inlands, the countryside is filled with birds, mammals, butterflies, and dragonflies— a bounty of wildlife to enjoy. In order to call attention to the many natural attractions throughout Raymondville, Port Mansfield, and Lyford, "Wild in Willacy" was created in 1999, and has continued every year since its magical beginnings. This festival was host to nationally renowned bird and butterfly field guides, and has purposed through the years to teach locals and visitors about such subjects as xeriscaping, and building bird and butterfly gardens. Access to private ranches is provided to the public once a year, and airboat rides into the sloughs of Port Mansfield offer birders rarely seen shorebirds that nest in the Laguna Madre. With Willacy being billed as "The Most Ecologically Diverse County in South Texas," visitors come from as far away as Canada to enjoy all that "Wild Willacy" has to offer.

RAYMONDVILLE

The ranching and farming community of Raymondville is the Willacy County seat, and the gateway to the Valley on U.S. 77, connecting the Valley to the Coastal Bend region of Texas. The flat, four-lane highway runs through Willacy County into Harlingen and then onto Brownsville. It was a town known at the turn of the century as "El Muerto," which means The Dead Man, and it has struggled through the years to survive. This nickname supposedly came about because of a story told by old timers of a man who lost his way and died in the dusty dry area. With the determination of townspeople to persevere, Raymondville survived the Great Depression and began to grow and prosper, (and thankfully began to lose the unpleasant nickname.) On your day in this friendly ranching town, be sure to visit the Raymondville Historical and Community Center where you will see dioramas portraying ranch life in the Valley. You'll also find exhibits of old ranching equipment and furnishings from Spanish land grant days up to the turn of the century. The Farm and Ranch Museum, which is adjacent to the Community Center, displays collections from local pioneer ranching families. The walls are covered in murals throughout, depicting the many wars in which Raymondville participated.

PORT MANSFIELD

Good lodging, restaurants, clubs, marinas, RV parks and great hunting and fishing have made Port Mansfield one of the sporting hot spots of the Valley, and it has earned the nickname, "angler's paradise." In fact, hunters and fishermen would really rather we keep it a secret! Too bad! Bordered by the King Ranch, this town was once a small commercial fishing village that serviced port for oil companies. Today, wading and pier fishing produce exciting fish tales, and an annual fishing tournament that is held each July. Port Mansfield is also one of two sites in the Valley with excellent conditions for scuba diving. Port Mansfield Liberty Ship Reef, located 15 miles off Port Mansfield, has become encrusted with invertebrates, such as corals and sponges, which attract grouper, snapper, amberjack, tarpon and shark—an ideal site for diving.

For more information on Raymondville, call the Raymondville Chamber of Commerce at 956-689-3171 or visit www.raymondvillechamber.com.

For more information on Port Mansfield, call the Port Mansfield Chamber of Commerce at 956-944-2354.

Raymondville / Port Mansfield Fairs Festivals & Fun

January
Willacy County Heritage Gala
Willacy County Livestock Show/Ranch Rodeo

February
Wild Game Tourist Appreciation Dinner

May
Young Farmers' Fishing Tournament

July
Fourth of July Festival
Port Mansfield Fishing Tournament

September
Riders and Ropers Youth Rodeo (Saturdays)

November
"Wild in Willacy" Nature Festival

December
Christmas Tree Lighting
Annual Christmas Parade

Serving Raymondville and Willacy County

When visiting a new town, the chamber of commerce is always the best place to start. All chambers hold great information and local secrets—the Raymondville Chamber of Commerce is no exception.

The friendly folks at the Raymondville Chamber of Commerce are happy to tell you about special events; offer directions; or provide you with brochures. Step into the Chamber for a calendar of events and step back in time by visiting the Raymondville Historical Museum and its newly created Costume Room. The Costume Room captures the era of World War I and II with authentic uniforms and grand ball gowns worn by the women of that time. The outside Museum walls tell stories through murals painted by local artists depicting the many wars of our nation.

The Raymondville Chamber of Commerce, 142 S. Seventh Street, offers activity ideas for visitors and locals. Let the staff help you and your family get the most out of your trip. Open Monday-Friday 8 am-4:30 pm. Call 956-689-3171.

Art, Fashion &Accessories

ARMANDO'S BOOT COMPANY

No one understands the importance of a good shoe better than the staff at Armando's Boot Company. The art of handcrafted boot-making has been passed down through generations of the Rios family, and now Armando Rios, (after working as an apprentice for 25 years), keeps the family tradition alive with his own boot company—Armando's. He is also passing on his knowledge to his son, Armando Duarte, Jr. He, too, is a gifted bootmaker.

Armando's Boot Company, 169 N. 7th Street in Raymondville, not only offers one of the best selections of brand names in the area, but also guarantees that his customers have the perfect fit every time. Each boot is specially made to fit the shape of each customer's foot. Whether your needs are for a wider boot or a more narrow style, Armando does everything possible to make sure you leave with the absolute best fit. You can choose from different types of leather, heels and toes, and opt for specialties such as initials. If you're in need of high-quality, custom made boots, and if you're looking for top service—search no further than Armando's Boot Company. You can't miss it. Just look for the giant boot on top of the building. Here, you can feel confident that your footwear will fit and feel fabulous.

Armando's Boot Company is open Monday-Friday 8 am-noon and 1-5 pm and Saturday 8 am-2 pm. To find out more about Armando's, call 956-689-3521.

Attractions,
Entertainment & Museums

Married couples Cesar and Dolores Nieto and Ernesto and Norma Hernandez always thought that their community needed a "nice place close to home where people could go and celebrate." Deciding they should be the ones to do something about it, these four friends opened Kasino Event Center, 1205 South 7th Street in Raymondville. Kasino Event Center's perfect for celebrations of all sizes and occasions!

In face, it's versatile enough for any event—dress it up for a wedding reception or if you like, make it more casual for a truly unforgettable birthday party. The owners and staff of the Kasino Event Center bend over backwards to cater to each clientele's needs, including making the center available to rent for an evening or simply by the hour. The Kasino Event Center is also ideal for business meetings and conferences—with plenty of room for presentations or even a business luncheon.

The facility, which includes a bar, a stage and a dance floor, and can accommodate up to 700 people, is equipped to host any event. Although in a dry area, the center is certified for their guests to B.Y.O.B. ("bring your own bottle"). For your next get-together, call the Kasino Event Center for an especially memorable time!

Regular business hours are Friday and Saturday; however, appointments are available to fit your schedule. For more information, call 956-571-2252.

Condominiums

SEASIDE RENTALS

In a town that is perfect for discovering the beauty of the outdoors, Seaside Rentals takes advantage of its prime location. With its fully-equipped condos, each Seaside rental offers a full kitchen stocked with the "day to day necessities," and a television. And, its 16 waterfront condos are all equipped with private docks and boat slips.

Located on 404 Bayshore in Port Mansfield, Seaside Rentals are in the perfect location for families and kids to walk around the town; watch the local wildlife of birds, hogs, turkey and deer; or visit the nearby park and fishing pier. Open everyday 8:30 am-5:30 pm. Call 956-944-2635.

Gifts & Home Décor

Coffee is just 10 cents a cup at the serve yourself coffee bar and gathering place at Watson's City Drug, 192 S. 7th Street. Once an old city theater, the building still exudes the charm and charisma of its past life. Watson's City Drug has been open since 1971, and although now owned by Matthew Kiefer, Mr. Watson is still one of the pharmacists.

Tradition and families are important here; many of the employees have been here for 10 or more years. The store is a favorite place to shop for jewelry, wedding gifts, cosmetics and beauty products. You'll find Claire Burke home fragrances, candles by Bridgewater, and treasures by Russ Berrie & Co. and Figi Graphics. Watson City Drug is a favorite bridal registry, too, because there are so many unique and wonderful items. The store is open Monday-Friday 8:30 am-7:30 pm, Saturday until 6 pm and Sunday until noon. Call 956-689-2161.

Restaurants &
Specialty Shops

MARGARET'S COUNTRY STORE

Once owning a beauty salon and a flower shop all in one, Margaret Fonseca still longed for more than her already distinctive shop. With the help of her husband, Mike, she was able to realize that dream by opening Margaret's Country Store and Pepper's Deli.

Bringing back the spirit of the all in one general store, Margaret has opened quite a treasure in her small town. Pepper's Deli offers an array of Boars Head meats and homemade pies and canned vegetables provided by local farmers, while the country store has everything from fresh flowers and antiques to a gallon of milk. Another charming aspect of Margaret's is that if you like something, even if it looks like part of the store's decoration, most likely, it's for sale.

Customers of this once sleepy town have come alive with the help of Margaret's Country Store and Pepper's Deli, 204 Broadway in Lyford. Margaret has helped bring the Old Fashioned charm back into this adorable town. A little bit of country charm with a twist of the new, and she and her family have found their niche—and Margaret never had to put down her scissors. If you're looking for the owner, chances are she's in the back giving another customer a haircut or making an arrangement.

Go in for a few groceries or a sandwich and leave with an antique desk for your study, some fresh flowers for a loved one, and a new haircut.

Hours are Monday-Saturday 9 am-7 pm and Sundays 11 am-3 pm. For more information, call 956-347-3031.

BOOT COMPANY BASKETS & GIFTS
BOOT COMPANY BAR & GRILL

At Boot Company Baskets and Gifts, owners Cruz and Sonya Tijerina offer a little something different than your standard gift shop. Along with a great selection of fashion accessories, linen outfits and unique gifts, the Tijerinas also serve up a great, tender steak and a menu full of other delicious dishes. Boot Company Baskets and Gifts has expanded from a place to shop to a bar and grill. However, even before the expansion, this place had a unique history.

Located at 205 E. Hidalgo Avenue in Raymondville, the Boot Company Baskets and Gifts building was once Rios Boot Company. Famous for its custom made boots, Rios Boot Company grabbed the attention and feet of such celebrities as former President Ronald Reagan, Prince Charles and King Hussein of Jordan. In fact, Rios Boot Company gave many of the boot makers across the Rio Grande their start. Some of the existing boot makers in the area are sons or relatives to former Rios Boot Company boot makers.

Customers of Boot Company Baskets and Gifts can learn more about the building's intriguing history through pictures, artifacts, and articles while browsing through the restaurant and shop.

Cruz and Sonya Tijerina's dream has expanded, letting you relax, have a drink, a great meal and then pick up a few things for your friends and family on the way out. Open Monday-Sunday 10 am-10 pm. Take advantage of this one-of-a-kind eatery and shop by calling 956-689-2668 or 956-689-3850.

Index

Cross Reference

Hotels / Motels / Condominiums
Alamo Inn – 65
Best Western Palm Aire Hotel & Suites – 158
Courtyard by Marriott – 78
Executive Inn & Suites – 106
Fairfield Inn & Suites, Weslaco – 157
Fairfield Inn and Suites by Marriott, McAllen – 79
Hilton Garden Inn – 78
Island Services – 128
La Borde House – 141
Marriott Courtyard – 50
Quality Inn – 129
Ramada Limited – 51
Residence Inn by Marriott – 20
Seaside Rentals – 167
Super 8 Motel – 51, VI
Texan Guest Ranch – 66
White Sands Motel & Marina – 130

Interior Design
Bugambilias Marketplace – 150
Cactus Flower Interiors – 124
Casa Antigua – 18, 72
Celina's Interiors – 71, V
Coun-Tree Woods – 45
Creative Interiors – 20
Decora Design – 124
Ele's Gift Shop & Cantera Rancho Alegre – 149
Glassica – 95
Glory B's – 47
Hacienda San Miguel – 70
Renee's of Sharyland – 101, Back Cover
Rustic Furniture Exclusive – 104
Sisters – 119
Sollet Unique Gifts & Crafts – 72
Veldany's Gifts – 76
Westgate Building Company – 158

Jewelry
Accents – 123
Antiques & Artisan Emporium – 38
Art~Local & Beyond – 120
Barn White – 73
Becky's Place – 126
Black Iris – 96
Deena's Gifts and Collectibles – 46
Dress Black – 79
Glory B's – 47
Jackson Street Antiques – 37
Jakybon Accessories – 80
Joyeria Daisy – 140
Lionel's Western Wear – 155
Margaret's Country Store – 168
Merle Norman Cosmetics – 109

Purple Parrot Gallery and Gift Shop – 120
Simply by Grace – 81
Simply Irresistible – 39
Sollet Unique Gifts & Crafts – 72
The Gift Garden – 102
The Silver Junction – 125
Watson's City Drug – 167

Museums
City of Hidalgo – 63
Frontera Audubon Society – 154, IV
Raymondville Chamber Of Commerce – 164
Weslaco Bicultural Museum – 151

Quilts
Picket Fence Quilt & Fabric Shop – 56
Simply Irresistible – 39

Realtors
Island Services – 128
Lynne Tate Real Estate, Inc. – 127, VI

Resorts
El Rocio Retreat Center – 97

Restaurants
All Time Snacks – 27
Boot Company Bar & Grill – 169
Chilé Piquin Café – 84
City Café & Catering – 84
Coffee Zone – 27
Deena's Gifts and Collectibles – 46
Dolphin Cove Oyster Bar – 130
El Patio Restaurant – 107
El Rocio Retreat Center – 97
Executive Inn & Suites – 106
Jack's Place – 52
Jose's Cafecito – 159
La Jaiba Shrimp House – 28
La Tejana Steakhouse – 108
Lee's Pharmacy – 77
Los Lagos Golf Club – 31
Margaret's Country Store – 168
Palmetto Inn – 132
Pirate's Landing – 131, VII
RB's Diner – 142
Renee's of Sharyland – 101, Back Cover
Sahadi Specialty Foods & Café – 85
Scampi's Restaurant & Bar – 132
Sea Ranch Restaurant – 131, VII
Simon's Deli – 52
Sweet Temptations – 86
The Blue Onion – 86, 159
The Blue Shell – 21, 88
The Club at Cimarron – 90, 98
White Sands Restaurant – 131

"A LADY'S DAY OUT GIVEAWAY"
ENTRY FORM

HAVE FIVE OF THE BUSINESSES FEATURED IN THIS BOOK SIGN YOUR ENTRY FORM AND YOU ARE ELIGIBLE TO WIN ONE OF THE FOLLOWING: WEEKEND GET AWAY AT A BED AND BREAKFAST, DINNER GIFT CERTIFICATES, SHOPPING SPREE GIFT CERTIFICATES OR $250 CASH.

1. _____
   (NAME OF BUSINESS)   (SIGNATURE)

2. _____
   (NAME OF BUSINESS)   (SIGNATURE)

3. _____
   (NAME OF BUSINESS)   (SIGNATURE)

4. _____
   (NAME OF BUSINESS)   (SIGNATURE)

5. _____
   (NAME OF BUSINESS)   (SIGNATURE)

NAME: _____

ADDRESS: _____

CITY: _____ STATE: _____ ZIP: _____

PHONE#: _____ E-MAIL: _____

WHERE DID YOU PURCHASE BOOK? _____

TEXAS TOWNS OR BUSINESSES YOU FEEL SHOULD BE INCORPORATED IN OUR NEXT BOOK. _____

NO PURCHASE NECESSARY. WINNERS WILL BE DETERMINED BY RANDOM DRAWING FROM ALL COMPLETE ENTRIES RECEIVED. WINNERS WILL BE NOTIFIED BY PHONE AND/OR MAIL.

MAIL TO: **FAX TO:**
A LADY'S DAY OUT   817-236-0033
8563 BOAT CLUB ROAD   PHONE: 817-236-5250
FORT WORTH, TX 76179   WEBSITE: www.aladysdayout.com